This is a Very Spe[cial]
for a
Very Special Person
namely
Patricia Wanner R.N
from
The author, Ben Holt
Age 95

THE OLD MAN ON THE CORNER
526 - 14th Street South
Zip 58102 ÷ Phone 235-8663

Finding Christ in the Old Testament

Finding Christ in the Old Testament

by
Benjamin M. Holt, LL.D.

VANTAGE PRESS
New York   Washington   Atlanta   Hollywood

FIRST EDITION

All rights reserved, including the right of reproduction in whole or in part in any form.

Copyright © 1977 by Benjamin M. Holt, LL.D.

Published by Vantage Press, Inc.
516 West 34th Street, New York, New York 10001

Manufactured in the United States of America
Standard Book Number 533-02825-6

Dedicated to Mrs. Petra C. Holt, the deceased wife of the author:

Just one more day for my Petra and me;
  Just one day more; that once more we might see;
Just one day more of God's mercy and peace;
  Just one day more; that our problems might ease.

The air was so fresh; the sun shone so bright;
  We sat by your side; by day and by night.
You hated to leave us; but God said: "No:
  Your time has now come; with Me you must go."

Your trials are over; your dark days are past;
  Your home in heaven is coming at last;
Your faith in your Savior brought you to God;
  The ransom was paid with Christ's precious blood.

God in His mercy has brought you to rest;
  He always arranged for your very best;
Some day your kind face again we'll behold;
  Walking together on streets of pure gold.

Just sixty-four years together we stayed;
  Just sixty-four years together we prayed;
Just sixty-four years; and what a great life;
  Just sixty-four years—a wonderful wife.

THE HOLTS on June 9, 1909

Contents

Eternity	1
The Book of Genesis	2
The Angel of the Lord, Whose Is He?	4
The Book of Exodus	17
The Book of Leviticus	19
The Book of Numbers	20
The Book of Deuteronomy	21
The Book of Joshua	22
The Book of Judges	23
The Book of Ruth	26
First Book of Samuel	26
The Second Book of Samuel	27
First Book of Kings	33
Second Book of Kings	34
First Book of Chronicles	35
The Second Book of Chronicles	36
The Book of Ezra	36
The Book of Nehemiah	36
The Book of Esther	37
The Book of Job	39
The Psalms	40
The Book of Proverbs	41
The Book of Ecclesiastes	41
What Does Predestination Really Mean?	42
The Songs of Solomon	45
The Book of Isaiah	46
The Book of Jeremiah	47

The Book of Lamentations	48
The Book of Ezekiel	51
The Book of Daniel	51
The Book of Hosea	52
The Book of Joel	53
The Book of Amos	53
The Book of Obadiah	54
The Book of Jonah	54
The Book of Micah	60
The Book of Nahum	61
The Book of Habakkuk	61
The Book of Zephaniah	62
The Prophet Haggai	62
The Book of Zechariah	63
The Book of Malachi	63
Immortality	66
Parables	69
Life Hereafter	72
Addenda	73
Time for Prayer	74

Finding Christ in the Old Testament

Eternity

By the word eternity we mean something that came, keeps on going, and will never stop; forever the same, no beginning and no end.

Somewhere, somehow within these eternal timeless and spaceless conditions, which in no way modify or restrict existence, we find also Christ (God), always and forever.

Man may be able to walk on the bottom of the ocean and dance on the top of the moon, but he will never be able to tell us what eternity really is, this inexplainable and inexpressible state of affairs, until some day when we shall meet Christ face to face.

Infinitely great and faultless, He is intelligent; a free *Being* of great goodness, wisdom and power, transcendently glorious in His holiness, He who made the universe, and continues to uphold and support it, as well governing and directing it by His own providence and laws. (Gen. 1,1-31; Ex. 7,16; 34,6; Deut. 33,27; Josh. 24,29; 1 Sam. 17,46; 2 Kings 19,15; 1 Chron. 17,24; Neh. 9,17; Ps. 5,4; 57,2; 12,2; Jer. 10,10.)

Christ, so the Scriptures tell us, IS from eternity, begotten by the Father in a special manner no creature ever was (and never will be); equal with the Father as a person, and *one* in Him in essence and indispensable quality.

The kingdom He was commissioned by the Father to establish was (and is) a spiritual and moral kingdom for the purpose of uniting the whole world by and within the ties of a confessional faith.

It was *"In The Beginning"* that Christ, together with the Father and the Spirit, CREATED the heaven and the earth

(Gen. 1,1). Cf. John 1,3. "ALL things were created by HIM; and without Him nothing was made" (John 1,2); when the *Word (Logas)* clearly shows Christ to be a preexisting person even *before* incarnation (Rev. 19,13). Cf. Isa. 34,10; Rev. 14,11.

"The Lord possessed me in the beginning... I was set up from everlasting... when He prepared the heavens. I was there... and was brought up with Him" (Prov. 8,22; 23,30). Cf. John 1,1. "And *He* is before all things, and by Him all things consist... equal with God" (Phil. 2,6). "And now, O Father, glorify Thou Me with Thine own self with the glory which I had with Thee *before* the world began" (John 17,5).

Christ then, from the beginning was, even all the way throughout the Old Testament, as we shall hereinafter see.

The Book of Genesis

Moses here gives us many things, among them a short record of creation and the origin of our universe, the human race, Sin, family life, the corruption of society at that time; and, believe it or not, also *Redemption* (Christ) (Gen.3,15). So you see we are off to a good start with *Finding Christ in the Old Testament*.

The matter of Creation of course comes under the fire of the modern critic, but when we consider that thirty-eight chapters have been given as an account and history of the chosen family, and only *one* chapter dealing with creation, then we must conclude that Moses took it for granted that we should *believe* what he said about creation, though we do not understand.

Yes, indeed, Moses *does* tell us about the Temptation and the Fall; about the personal character of Satan and the singularity of sin; so we might as well begin right from the start and talk about *Law and Gospel* (although I will repeat this at a later time). (Gen. 3,15; 17,17,19.) Cf. John 7,42.

Moses involves everything from creation to the end of the world in two words, Sin and Redemption, which leads us right into *Law and Gospel*. And what is there, really, that leads us along the path that gains for us heaven aside from *Law and Gospel?* That is, confession and forgiveness, sin and grace? Throughout the entire Old Testament is there actually anything at all beyond pardon and peace, should we say sorrow over sin and hope of reconciliation?

How much is there to Law and Gospel except confession and forgiveness? The Law simply exposes to us God's fierceness and fury, and reveals to us our thoughts and deeds and secret sins thrown in for good measure, and thus becomes for us an expression of imminent danger and potential penalty for violation of God's rules and what He expects of us.

The Gospel (Gen. 3,15; Gen. 3,17,19) on the other hand shows us the antithetical side of the Law, and makes evident by Scriptural procedure that regardless of our sins, be they great or small, there IS hope and forgiveness for all who confess their sins and accept (receive without doubt) the Son of God as their Lord and Savior.

And, this forgiveness and pardon on the part of God is granted to us without any merit or excellence whatever on our part.

Most of us have, during out lives, received some sort of "Award of Merit," and a pat on the back for work well done. But redemption (the Gospel) knows of no rewards for conduct; no competitive examinations are permitted. Eternal life is *free*.

But, now comes the difficult (hard to understand) part: The Law and the Gospel go hand in hand, always. We just cannot have the one without the other. They come in pairs!

To begin with we must understand and admit that repentance and forgiveness (sin and grace) were the fundamental essence of Christ's entire ministry on earth. Oh yes, there was concentration and fragrance in every word that He spoke; blessings and pleasure in every act that He performed. But NOT without repentance (Matt. 3,2; Mk.1,15; Luke 17,3,5).

All this is confirmed even before Christ was born (Num. 23,19). Cf. Ex. 13, 17; 32, 12; Deut. 32, 36; Job 42,6; Jer. 18,8; 26, 18. The Law and Gospel are clearly made mainfest in both the Old and the New Testaments; and they are in no way contentious—the one does not try to argue with the other.

The *Law* commands, demands, requires, requests and makes accusations and charges against us; whereas the *Gospel* supplies, provides, compensates, makes good, and shows us Christ, not only as He suffered, died and rose again, but it also gives us a true picture of His glory and splendor, where He is NOW seated on the right hand of the Father.

True, the Law does promise a way out *if* you do this and/or do not do that. But the Gospel has no "IF's," but brings us a proclamation that not only offers but BRINGS forgiveness and pardon, and actually takes away all desires and justifiable intensities on the part of God to let the Law take its course.

So, when it comes to a vindication and defense act before God, *then* the Law becomes wholly inoperative and ineffective (Isa. 34, 25; 43, 22; 55,7; Ezek. 26,25; Mic. 7,18; 1 John 1,9).

The Angel of the Lord, Who Is He?

As before stated, Moses has presented to us in one word (Seed) the only real plan of salvation, and made special efforts to acquaint us with God's Divine Covenent (Gen. 2,9). Cf. Gen. 3,22; Ps. 51, 5-13, which in turn leads us face to face with the Doctrine of Justification by Faith without the deeds of the Law; as he relates to us the story of Cain and Abel, whose parents (Adam and Eve) bear testimony as to what (and why) happened in the Garden of Eden; and, that *Faith*, not works, is pleasing to God (Gen. 4,4). Cf. Job 5,8; Eccl. 5, 2.

Justify not thyself lest God be angry (Job 32, 2), but take delight in approaching God (Isa. 58, 2). And if you please, and be patient, we shall make every effort, based on Biblical proofs, to show you that Christ is to be found over and over again throughout the Old Testament, also in the form of *The Angel of the Lord;* to wit:

The Angel of the Lord

These theses will deal directly with the Old Testament—"Angel of The Lord." Who is He, and Why? Scripture mentions "The Angel of the Lord" some forty-two times in general, and some twenty-seven times specifically.

The question then arises: Is He one of the good angels, that is, one of the obedient messengers of God (Hebr. 1,14); or perhaps one of the unseen citizens of heaven carrying out the orders of The Most High (Ps. 104, 4)?

Might He be one of the seven archangels (Jewish history) or one of the four archangels (1 Thes. 4,16), or could it be that His name is "Gabriel," the angel who comforted Daniel and gave him great wisdom (Dan. 8,15-27), the very same angel who announced the conception of John the Baptist (Luk. 1,19-25) and also told Mary to name her son "JESUS" (Luk. 1,30-31)?

Would you say, off hand, that "The Angel of the Lord" might be "Michael," the angel who argued with Satan over the body of Moses (Jude 9), and also won the war in heaven at the time the devil and all his evil companions were cast out forever (Rev. 12, 7-9)?

Then there are also the various "groups" of angels, such as Thrones, Dignities, Powers, Authorities, Dominions, Principalities, etc. (Eph. 1,21; 1 Pet. 3, 22; 2 Pet. 2, 11; Jude, 8). Might "The Angel of the Lord" belong to one or more of these groups; or might He be one of *"The Holy Ones of God"* (Luk. 9, 26)?

Or could it be possible that "The Angel of the Lord" is one of the Cherubims at God's side (Isa. 37, 16) who also guarded the gate to the Garden of Eden at the time of the fall (Gen. 3, 24), or a member of the glorious order of Seraphim (Isa. 6,1-2; Ezek. 10, 3)?

To all these questions the answer is No. "The Angel of the Lord" does not come under any of the foregoing classifications. He is an *Angel of His Own Making;* of which we shall learn a great deal as we go along with our research.

There is much that we could (and should) learn by studying the actual ministry, office, and duties of God's angels. One thing we may be sure of, very sure, and that is that one or more of them watches over us day and night (Mark, 1,-13; Dan. 6,22).

The angels are *Created Beings* (Col. 1,16); have great knowledge but are not omniscient (Mk. 13,32), and they are not proper subjects to be worshipped (Hebr. 1, 6; 1 Pet. 3, 22;) but are bidden to worship Christ and are under His supervision (Eph. 1, 10; 3, 15).

The angels—they speak, they hear, they see, they feel; but this does not go to say that they require an actual *visible* body in order to establish their personal individuality.

They are fully cognizant of the majesty and profundity of Divine Council, and thus they continually grow in knowledge regarding God's eternal plan of salvation (1 Pet. 1, 12; Eph. 3, 10).

The angels have, as an attribute, unlimited capacity and capability of power (Rev. 20, 1-3), and even the *Law* was given through angels (Gal. 3,19; Acts 7, 53; Hebr. 2, 2); so *important are they!*

So before we go any further let us try to distinguish between "The Angel of the Lord" of the Old Testament and angels in general.

For instance, when an angel came to rescue Paul and opened the prison doors (Acts 5,19); or, when an angel delivered Peter out of the hands of his enemies (Acts 12, 1-17); or, an angel caused the wretched body of King Herod to be eaten up by worms (Acts 12, 23)—these were all acts performed by a *created* angel (or angels).

Now there has been (and is) a great deal of variation in the interpretation of Scripture as to *WHO* "The Angel of the Lord" is. However, it is universally accepted that "The Angel of the Lord" is none other than Angel of The Old Testament, the Pre-Incarnate Son of God, The Second Person of the Trinity, in short, God Himself (with the Father).

Let us remember also that this pre-incarnate union of God with humanity does *not* begin even in the Garden of Eden (Gen. 3, 15), when our Lord said to the Serpent: "I will put enmity between you and the woman, and between you and her *Seed*"; but dates back to *before the world began* (John 1,1; 1 John 3,7).

Here are the Old Testament references as to how and when "The Angel of the Lord" eternal appeared. One of the first Scripture passages in question is when He came to Hagar, the betrayed Egyptian maid-servant of Sarah, mother of Ishmael.

1) Hagar had been cast out and forsaken by Abraham's enraged wife, and while thus grief stricken and suffering from want in the wilderness, "The Angel of the Lord" came to her in person to comfort and console her (Gen. 16, 1-16).

2) Then again when Abraham sat in his tent in the grove near Hebron, "The Angel of the Lord" came to him (in the form of a man) and promised him that Sarah, who was far beyond the age of bearing children, should give birth to a son, the which turned out to be none other than Isaac (Gen. 18, 1-4; 21, 1-3).

3) One evening around the year 1898 B.C. there came two angels to Lot to warn him of the destruction of the city. Lot calls them "My Lords." His enemies called one of them "Fellow," which is also a name so often given to the Son of God. See also 2 Kings 9,11; Matt. 12, 24; 26, 61; Luk. 23, 2; Zech. 13, 7, which all leads us right back to the Messianic Prophecies in Gen. 3, 15 and Mal. 3, 1 (Gen. 19, 1-21).

4) At the time Abraham was to offer up his son Isaac as a burnt offering, "The Angel of the Lord" came to him and said: "Lay not thy hand upon the lad" (Gen. 22, 1-12).

5) While Jacob was in trouble at Bethel "The Angel of the Lord" spoke to him in a dream and said: "Lift up your eyes, and see... I AM the God of Bethel... where thou made a vow *onto Me* (Gen. 31, 11-13. See also Gen. 28, 10-22). Covenants and vows are made with *God;* but not with angels.

6) There was a small rivulette that had its source in the Hauran Mountains and emptied into River Jordan, called Jabbok. In his fear over Esau's attack Jacob sent his household (family) across the river, and while he was there alone, "The Angel of the Lord" (a man) came to Jacob, with whom he wrestled all night (Gen. 32, 34).

7) While Joseph was visiting his father who was ill, Jacob

stretched out his arms over his grandsons Manasseh and Ephraim and blessed them in God's name, he refers to Christ as "The Angel which redeemed me from all evil." Now we all know that no uncreated angel can *redeem* only the Son of God "redeemeth the soul of his servants" (Ps. 34, 22); only He who did *create* (Gen. 1, 1) can preserve thy soul (Ps. 121, 7). In verse 3 he calls Him "God Almighty" (Gen. 48, 1-16).

8) When Moses was herding his father-in-law's sheep, "I AM" appeared to him in a flame of fire out of the midst of a bush. Later Jehovah Himself spoke directly to Moses who had to hide his face from His Holy Countenance, so bright and glorious was it. It was then that Jehovah (God) said to Moses: "Say unto the children of Israel, I AM hath sent me unto you." As we know "I AM" Is also one of the titles or names given to Christ, see John 8, 58. "Image of God," 2 Cor. 4, 4. (Ex. 3, 1-14).

9) While Israel was preparing to cross the Red Sea "The Angel of the Lord" went before them and brought them safely across (Ex. 19, 22).

10) At the time Moses made provisions for Moses to "cut off," little by little, the entire nations of the Hittites, the Perizzites, the Canaanites, the Hivites, and the Jebusites, He sent HIS ANGEL to lead Israel and to bring His people safe into the place He had prepared for them, which consisted of all the land from the Red Sea to the Philistine Sea and from the desert country all the way over to the river country.

This "His Angel" (v. 23) God calls "Mine Angel"; very special, for He has the power to "forgive" sin and to "pardon transgressions (v. 21); and with This Angel, the Son and the Father are *united;* for they have *always been one;* even since times eternal (Ex. 23, 20-31).

11) When the people caused Aaron to make them a calf of gold (an idol) for them to worship, both Moses (and God) became very angry. This was a most terrible sin on the part of Israel, so God threatened to strike the names of all those who so had sinned out of the Book of Heaven. But even *then* God went along with Moses so that He sent His Angel, "Mine Angel," to go before them, although He did punish them later (Ex. 32, 1-35).

12) While the Egyptians were giving Moses a bad time on his way from Kadesh to Mount Hor, God again sent *His Angel* (Divine Leader) to go before them (Num. 20, 15-22).

13) Balaam, a prophet, and a son of Beor, though in his own way he worshipped Jehovah, he also taught false doctrines, and practiced forbidden arts and divinations. He also had the habit of betraying people for reward. So God finally got very angry with him because of his disobedience.

It was then that "The Angel of the Lord" appeared on the scene, and stood before Balaam and the ass upon which he was riding. Balaam at first did not see "The Angel of the Lord," and thus he tried several times to force his donkey to proceed ahead.

When Balaam finally saw "The Angel of the Lord" he fell flat on his face to the ground, and also confessed his many sins, and God made all things good again.

No one absolves sin but God, in this case "The Angel of the Lord," the Second Person of the Holy Trinity, and this before a man who knew less than an animal (Num. 22, 22-34).

14) After "The Angel of the Lord" had brought the Israelites out of Egypt He made a solemn *covenant* with the people. He came all the way up from Gilgal to Bochim to remind them that there should be NO IDOLATRY, and that all the heathen altars should be demolished. But the people did not obey "The Angel of the Lord." Their punishment was that their enemies should remain in the land and become a real thorne in their flesh, and that their idols should be a dangerous snare unto them. Then they wept (Judg. 2, 1-5).

15) While Joshua was at Jericho "a man" stood over him with a drawn sword in His hand. And this "man" was none other than "The Lord of Hosts" for so He called Himself. Joshua fell on his face to the ground and did WORSHIP Him, calling Him *My Lord.*"

And just WHO could this "man" be other than the preincarnate Son of God, Jesus Himself? Is He not also called "Man of God's right hand" (Ps. 80, 17); Mighty God (Isa. 9, 6); Lord of Hosts (Isa. 54, 5); Lord of Righteousness (Jer. 23, 6); Lord, your Redeemer (Isa. 43, 14). The reference is Josh. 5, 13.

16) In "The Song of Deborah and Borak" (Judg. 5), "The Angel of the Lord" ordered Israel to call down God's wrath upon Meroz, a place of refuge in Northern Palestine, and to bitterly *curse* the inhabitants thereof because they refused to fight on the side of the Lord. And just *who* has the right to give such orders accept the Captain of the Lord of Hosts, as we read in Josh. 5, 14 (Judg. 5, 23; Mal. 2, 2; Ps. 37, 22).

17) The children of Israel did evil in the sight of God, so He delivered them into the hands of Midian (it was the Midianites who bought Joseph at a bargain). The Medianites too had joined Moab against Israel.

There were robberies, grasshoppers, humiliations, until one day "The Angel of the Lord" came and seated Himself under an oak tree close to where Gideon was threshing wheat. It was then that Gideon called Him "My Lord." It was later during their conversation that God promised Gideon that he would win the war and "smite the Midianites as one man" (Judg. 6, 1-16).

18) Manoah's wife (Judg. 13, 2), like Sarah (Gen. 11, 30), and Rebekah (Gen. 25, 21), and Rachel (Gen. 29, 31), and The Shumanite women (2 Kings 2, 14), and Hannah (1 Sam. 1, 2) and Elizabeth (Luk. 1, 2), was barren, and by nature could have no children except by a miracle.

So one day "The Angel of the Lord" came to her and said: "Just don't worry, I'll see to it that you give birth to a child; but he shall be a Narzarite (set apart for God forever), all the days of his life. And he (your son) shall begin to save your people from the hands of the wicked hands of the Philistines.

Manoah's wife told her husband all about this, and said this "man" who had talked to her looked like an Angel of God, and caused her to fear and tremble. When Manoah pleaded with God to confirm what his wife had told him, "The Angel of the Lord" appeared the second time to his wife.

Later when Manoah came in from the field, he too met "The Angel of the Lord," and asked Him if He was the "man" his wife had been talking to, and "The Angel of the Lord" said "I AM." I think I have mentioned in the foregoing too that "I AM" is one of the 256 names given to our Lord Jesus Christ in Holy Writ (Ex.

3, 1-14), "Him that dwelleth in the bush" (Deut. 33, 16) in a "flame of fire" (Acts 7, 30), Christ, who *is the Image of God* (2 Cor. 4, 4).

But Manoah also did not know who "The Angel of the Lord" was, so he asked Him what His name was, and while Manoah and his wife were going to offer up a burnt offering for Him he suddenly ascended to heaven in the flame that came up from this altar, and Manoah and his wife fell flat on their faces to the ground.

In due time Manoah's wife gave birth to a baby boy, none other than Samson, later for twenty years one of the Judges of Israel—classed as one of the heroes of the faithful (Judg. 13, 1-25).

19) David too had seriously offended the Lord, and was in great trouble, as was also his entire nation. Indeed so *much* was God displeased with them that He sent a great epidemic, and seventy thousand men died therefrom.

It was during David's pleading for mercy that the "The Angel of the Lord" (though He had come to destroy all of Jerusalem), that God, as usual with sinners, said to His Angel: *This is enough—stay your hand!* (1 Chron. 21, 14-30).

20) Elijah, the great prophet and reformer, though he possessed great wisdom and miraculous power from on high, he had to go through a multitude of trials and temptations, like all other children of God have to do.

At the time the wicked "witch" Jezabel (Rev. 2, 20; 2 Kings 9, 22), wife of the King of Tyre had threatened Elijah, he fled to Beersheba; and while there in the wilderness, seated under a Juniper tree begging God that he might die, he fell asleep, and "The Angel of the Lord" no doubt had provided him with a good breakfast, he did eat, but then he went back to bed.

Later "The Angel of the Lord" came to him the second time and touched him again, and said: Eat and drink and be on your way; great responsibilities face you!

Elijah then proceeded to Mount Hared (Mt. Sinai), and while there he ate no more food for forty days and forty nights (1 Kings 19, 1-8).

21) Ahaziah, like his father Ahab, worshipped idols. He was

seriously ill, and sent for messengers from the King of Samaria to consult Baalzebub, the idol of the Philistines and the god of Ekron, to inquire about his recovery.

In the meantime "The Angel of the Lord" came to Elijah, the prophet, and told him to intercept these messengers, and to remind them most forcefully that *Jehovah was still God of Israel.* And Ahaziah died, as "The Angel of the Lord" had predicted.

This enraged the enemy to a point where they sent a battalion of 50 men with two captains against Elijah, but Elijah brought fire down from heaven to consume them all.

It was then that "The Angel of the Lord" came to Elijah the second time and told him to come down from his hilltop refuge, and be afraid no more (2 Kings 1, 1-15).

22) Hezekiah, King of Judah, purged his nation of idolatry and restored the true form of worship acceptable of Jehovah.

When Sennacharib's extremely vulgar and blasphemous letter came to Hezekiah there soon was trouble in the air.

Hezekiah appealed to Isaiah who comforted and quieted him by assuring him that Sennacharib's armies should not prevail against him. Actually, *that very night* "The Angel of the Lord" went into the camp of the Asyrians and, behold, He slew 185,000 men, all found dead in the morning.

So what could Sennacharib do but return to his own land in shame, subsequently to be slain by his own sons (2 Kings 19, 1-35; 2 Chron. 32, 17-21); and thus the Lord again put a hook in the nose and a bridle in the mouth of all who blaspheme and speak sacrilegiously against God (Isa. 37, 8-29).

23) Another very suitable title given to the pre-incarnate Son of God in the Old Testament is: "The Angel of HIS Presence" (Isa. 63, 9). Let us spend a few lines in earnest conversation about this *Angel of (in) His (God's) Presence:*

In Kings James version we read as follows: In all their affliction He (the Angel) was (also) afflicted, and the ANGEL OF HIS PRESENCE "saved" them; in His love and in His pity He "redeemed" them; and He bare them, and carried them all the days of old (Isa. 63, 9).

In the RSV version we read: In all their affliction He (the

Angel) did not afflict, and THE ANGEL OF GOD'S PRESENCE "saved" them; in His love and His pity He "redeemed" them; He lifted them up and carried them all the days of old (Isa. 63, 9).

But here comes something real interesting: In the new (1963) edition of the Douay version we read: "They are indeed MY people, children who are not disloyal; so He [THE ANGEL] became their SAVIOR [see Deut. 4, 27ff] in every affliction. It was not a messenger or an angel [a created angel], but He [the Son of God] HIMSELF who saved them. Because of His love and pity He REDEEMED them HIMSELF, lifting them and carrying them all the days of old (Isa. 63, 8-9).

No "messenger" of God nor any created angel can "SAVE." None can "REDEEM," NO ONE, except THE SON OF GOD, whom we have so often referred to heretofore as "The Angel of The Lord."

Only He, the SECOND PERSON OF THE GODHEAD, One of Three yet Three in One, can rescue and preserve a world steeped in sin. Only HE can recover and PAY our old and long past due and forfeited account with the GREAT BOOKKEEPER ABOVE (Isa. 63, 9).

24) When Shadrach, Meshach and Abednego refused to fall down and worship the golden image (idol) set up by King Nebuchadnezzar, they were bound, hand and foot, and thrown into a specially heated fiery furnace seven times hotter than usual.

Later when the flames were flying and the furnace was roaring King Nebuchadnezzar peeked around the corner to see what had happened, and BEHOLD, right in the midst of the flames he saw, not only the three men, but he saw four men, all loose, and walking around as if nothing had happened (and nothing had happened). They were all alive and unhurt.

What puzzled the king was this: WHO WAS THIS FOURTH PERSON? Yes, it was "The Angel of the Lord," and Nebuchadnezzar said, he "WAS LIKE THE SON OF GOD."

There were many witnesses as to what had happened, since not even as much as a hair on their head, had been singed, neither did they smell of the smoke.

It was then that Shadrach, Meshach and Abednego thanked

God for sending them HIS ANGEL to deliver them (Dan. 3, 12-28).

25) When King Darius ruled the land Daniel was also cast into prison for saying his daily prayers, which was forbidden by the king. But God's ANGEL delivered Daniel from the mouths of the fierce lions, without a scratch. It was then that Daniel said: "O King, live forever. My God hath sent HIS ANGEL, and hath shut the lions' mouth" (Dan. 6, 9, 21).

26) Zechariah too mentions "The Angel of the Lord" several times. He himself talked with Him; he heard Him speak to others; he even heard Him speak to His Father in heaven, and also heard His Father's answer.

Furthermore, Zechariah was witness to Joshua's appearance before "The Angel of the Lord" while Satan was resisting him, which ANGEL was God's own Son the "BRANCH,"—"the MAN," (Zech. 3, 1-8; 6, 12).

27) Even the very last Book of the Old Testament (Mal. 3, 1) mentions "The Angel of the Lord," and refers to Him as the "MESSENGER OF THE COVENANT," the Covenant of Grace, called the Covenant of Redemption, namely the EVERLASTING COVENANT in which God the Father and God the Son engage to accomplish the salvation of mankind through the PERSON and the WORK of the Messiah.

And by and through THIS Covenant all other Covenants become relatively incidental, so that by the eternal priesthood of Christ even all the Levitical priesthoods of Aaron are abolished (Hebr. 9) for today CHRIST ALONE IS OUR SAVIOR, "The Angel of the Lord" and Incarnate Son of God, and we are His PEOPLE INDEED, FOREVER (Hebr. 8, 10).

Would you now dare to say that Christ is NOT to be found in the Old Testament?!

Moses now continues with the geneaology of the thirteen Patriots, ages from 807 to 1123 years, and the fate of Enoch who walked with God 365 years, and then was exempted from death, for "God took him" (Gen. 5, 24). Read now also about Elijah who went up to heaven in a whirlwind (2 Kings 2,11). Cf. Hebr. 11,5.

In this connection may we also mention the fact that Christ too was not exempted from dying, but He *did* rise upwards to heaven *with His own Power.* (More about Resurrection elsewhere.)

Moses also tells us about God's bitter anger over the sins of the people (His people); the subsequent flood when every human being and all animals and every living thing was utterly destroyed; God's second covenant (the rainbow in heaven); Noah's sin; the career of Abraham (third reference to the *Seed* (Christ); (Gen. 22,18; 26,4) and Abraham's potential possession of the Holy Land; the test of Abraham's obedience when he was asked to offer up his own son Isaac on the altar, typical of the subsequent sacrifice of the Son of God on Calvary (Gen. 22, 1-18). Cf. Gen. 17,19; 21,12; 28,14; and, "*Seed* of a woman" (Gen. 3,15). Cf. Isa. 7,14.

Many great men lived and died during the oncoming years, and Moses gives us a recap of Mankind Ruined; Paradise Lost; and Heaven Regained for all believers—Christ for every age, and Christ on every page (also for all Old Testament people who waited for His coming).

But right now, before we proceed, let us ponder a few facts in retrospect: In these days of high power, speed, love of wisdom and technological productivity, man has arrived at a point where he almost would like to take God apart and see what He is made of!

He believes nothing beyond that which is produced or exists in nature, and consequently he denies all the events of Creation as stated in God's Word (Gen. Chapters 1 and 2).

The thought and theory that man began with some sort of an animal life, and by processes of evolution and hereditary transmission of "slight" variations in successive generations lost both fin, feather and tail, and then turned into a human being, is a sad subject that begins in our high schools and ends up in our universities and (even) in our theological institutions and seminaries as a "fact."

The Scriptures tell us that *Christ* created heaven and all things (John 1,2). Have ye not heard that *He* who made them from the beginning "made them male and female," free from sin, *In His Own Image* (Gen. 1,27, 5,2); and that "for this cause shall (man) leave his own father and mother" (Gen. 2,24).

Herein (Christ *knew* Scriptures) Christ testifies to the fact that He *did accept*, not only the actualities of God's creative ability and power, but He *defends* marriage and the institution of the home as a most reliable entity and upholds individual existence as realism. Cf. Matt. 19, 3-9; Mk. 2,15; Gen. 5,2.

In Chapters 5 and 6, Moses tells us about the wickedness of the world; how Noah found grace before God; his building of the ark; how Noah's family as believers entered in; the beginning of the great (sin) flood, the increase of rainfall, when the fountains of the deep and the windows of heaven were finally shut off at God's command; how Noah and his family came forth out of the Ark, and built an altar and offered up sacrifices to God.

The entire story of the Ark and Noah is pure hokum and bunk to the intellectuals of our day. In fact one of these "Leaders of Mankind" says that "there was not even room for the manure of the animals in the Ark much less room for the animals."

But what did Christ say about this?

In relation to His Second Coming and the End of the World Christ *did say this:* "As the days of Noah were, SO shall also the Coming of the Son of Man be. For as the days were before the Flood, they were eating and drinking, marrying and giving in marriage, until the day that Noah entered into the Ark. And knew not until the Flood came and took them all away. So shall also the Coming of the Son of Man be" (Matt. 24,37-39; Luk. 17,26).

And hear this also: While in the wilderness Israel bitterly complained about the treatment God had provided for them. So God sent them fiery serpents to bite them, and many of them died. But when they subsequently repented of their sin, then God told Moses to make a fiery serpent and set it upon a pole, so that when anyone who had been bitten, as soon as they looked at the serpent on the pole, *they did not die* (Num. 21,8,9).

Quite often when Christ appealed for support He turned to "Moses and the Prophets" to prove His point; and this He did also in the case of the fiery serpent on the pole. Said Christ: "And as Moses lifted up the serpent in the wilderness, even so must the Son of Man be lifted up; that whosoever believeth in Him should not perish, but have eternal life" (John 3,14,15). "And I, if I be lifted up from the earth, will draw all men unto Me. THIS He said, signifying what death He should die" (John 12,32,33).

Then the question again comes up—*Whom shall we believe;* God's Word or man's nonsense?

The Book of Exodus

In the Book of Exodus we are told about the history of Israel from the time of Joseph to the building of the Tabernacle, the *key* thought being *"Deliverance."*

The book has four distinct divisions, 1) The period of bondage as well as the birth, and adoption and marriage of Moses. 2) The period of Deliverance; Moses at the burning bush; his companionship with Aaron; the ten plagues; and the *Passover*. 3) The period of discipline; the Exodus; and instructions for the journey, and the vast experiences on the way. 4) The period of legislation and reorganization; their arrival at Sinai; the appearance of God on the mountain; the Ten Commandments; the worship of the Golden Calf and its consequences.

The entire Pilgrimage of Israel can be summed up in one word, "Christ." The Egyptian bondage presents to us a type of the bondage of sin, Moses as Deliverer being a type of Christ; for instance, both were rescued in childhood (Ex. 2, 2-10; + Matt. 2,14,15); both had to battle Satan (Ex. 7,11 + Matt. 4,1); both fasted forty days (Ex. 34, 28 + Matt. 4,2); both had control of the sea (Ex. 14, 21 + Matt. 8, 26); both fed the multitudes (Ex. 16, 15 + Matt. 14,20,21); both had radiant faces (Ex. 34, 35 + Matt. 17,2); both were deserted in the home (Num. 12,1 + John 7, 5); both made intercessory prayers (Ex. 32, 32 + John 17, 9); both spoke as oracles (Deut. 18, 18 + John 4, 25; 8, 28; 17,8); both had seventy helpers (Num. 11, 16,17 + Luk. 10,1); both established memorials (Ex. 12,14 + Luk. 22, 19); and both reappeared after death (Matt. 3 + Acts 1,3).

We might even go on with types, as for instance: The Exodus in itself as a type of the departure from sin; The Passover Lamb, a type of Christ the Lamb of God; Pharaoh's pursuit of Israel, a type of the evil forces pursuing believers; the opening of the Red Sea, a type of Christ coming to our rescue; the pillar of cloud and fire, a type of the Divine Presence at all times for us; the Song of Moses, a type of our singing our songs of victory day by day; the mixed multitudes, a type of the worldly elements in our church today; manna, a type of Christ, the Bread of Life; the water from the rock, a type of Christ, the Living Water; the holding up of the hands of Moses, a type of the need we have for cooperation between Christians.

Besides, as we look at the structure of the Tabernacle, as a whole, its furniture, the ordinances, the garments of the priesthood, the ark of the covenant, etc., we also find many types of Christ and His Church.

And we must NEVER forget that through Christ, typically, enters the Israeli picture as the Lamb of God (Lev. 23,9); the Festival of the holy Passover (as it was written in the *Book of the Covenant*) was continued on through the days of Joshua (Josh. 5,10); Cf. 2 Kings 23,21; 2 Chron. 30,13; Ez. 6,19; and *was kept and observed by Christ Himself* (Matt. 26,19; Mk. 14,12; Luk. 22,7; 22,19).

"Having loved His own which were in the world, He loved them unto the end" (John 13,1). Cf. Luk. 22, 19; Matt. 26, 26; Mk. 14, 22.

Let's go one step further by associating our Lord and Savior (Redeemer) with *"The Angel [CHRIST] which redeemed me from all evil"* (Gen. 48,16). Cf. Gen. 31,11. "I AM the Lord, and I will bring you out from underneath the burdens of the Egyptians, and I will rid you of their bondage, and I will *Redeem* you with a stretched out arm" (Ex. 6,6). Cf. Ex. 15,13; Deut. 7,8; 1 Chron. 17,21; Neh. 1,10.

"Thou in Thy Mercy hast led forth the people which Thou hast Redeemed" (Ex. 15,13). Cf. Jer. 2,6; Isa. 63, 12, 13. No one except Christ can Redeem!

The Book of Leviticus

This BOOK is called the "Holy Book"; the word holy appears eighty times within its pages; its theme being: "THE WAY TO GOD."

But how can sinful man approach a God that is so holy that even the stars in the heavens melt with shame in His sight? The answer was then and is now, only through the *High Priest* (Christ); and the *key word* in the book is *"Access"* (admittance) to God, through sacrifices, 1) burnt offerings, signifying *Atonement*; 2) through meat offerings, signifying thanksgiving; 3) peace offerings, signifying fellowship with God; 4) sin offerings, signifying reconciliation; and 5) trespass offerings, signifying a cleansing from guilt.

Special enactments too were made to govern Israel, as to food, cleanliness, sanitation, customs, morals, etc., all of which was intended to emphasize purity of life as a condition of Divine favor.

There were five Feasts or annual Solemnities, 1) The Feast of the Passover commemorating the Exodus (going away); 2) The Feast of Pentecost, commemorating the giving of the Law; 3) The Feast of the Trumpets, when the high priest honored the New Year; 4) The Day of Atonement, when the Holy of Holies was entered for the purpose of atoning for the sins of the people; and 5) The Feast of the Tabernacle, commemorating the life spent in the wilderness.

Then there were the general enactments such as 1) The Sabbatical year (once in seven years), when the land was all left untilled; 2) The Year of Jubilee (once in fifty years) when all the slaves were set free, and all debts cancelled, and a series of warnings concerning chastisement was issued.

Finally: the Day of Atonement and the Feast of the Tabernacle is something we as Christians should *really* take seriously, *because* the Atonement and Atoning Acts are the Central Facts of the entire Old Testament sacrificial system; and Jesus Himself (The Promised *Seed*) declared that He gave His life as a ransom for many; for all; and He repeatedly appealed to the Law and the Prophets to back up everything that He said, did and taught!

The Book of Numbers

The book deals with the pilgrimage of Israel, its chief lesson being that unbelief closes the entrance to heaven. Cf. Hebr. 3, 7-19.

Some of the leading topics of the book are 1) legislation; 2) the Israelites' departure from Sinai; 3) their loathing of Manna; 4) quails for food; 5) the seventy elders appointed; 6) Miriam's and Aaron's jealousy; etc.

Then came the failures: 1) the report from the spies; 2) the rebellion of the people; 3) forty years of wandering in the wilderness; 4) the sin of Moses and the death of Aaron; 5) the brazen serpent and salvation attached thereto (Num. 21,9). "And as Moses lifted up the serpent in the wilderness, even so *must* the Son of Man be lifted up, that whosoever believeth in Him should not perish, but have eternal life" (John 3, 14,15).

While on the subject of Christ, let us also note these Messianic types: 1) The Smitten Rock (Num. 20, 7-11 and 1 Cor. 10,4); 2) The City of Refuge (Num. 35 and Hebr. 6,18).

As outlined in the foregoing we have much to learn also from this book, but the main thing is that Christ can be *and is* abundantly found all through the Old Testament.

Then also a word about the *"Sceptre"*; which *"shall not depart from Judah; nor a lawgiver from between his feet until Shiloh come"* Gen. 49;10. Cf. Num. 24,17; "A *star* out of Jacob" He is. Cf. Matt. 2,2. Christ, the "morning star," who brought us the Light of the Gospel.

"Thy throne, O God, is forever and ever; the Sceptre of Thy kingdom is a right Sceptre" (Ps. 45, 6).

The Book of Deuteronomy

This book gets its name from two Greek words: *deuteros;* meaning second; and *nomus;* meaning law—in other words, The Giving of the Law the second time.

Old Israel now had died in the wilderness, and therefore it was very important that the law should again be expounded before the new generation entered The Promised Land. The entire law was rehearsed time and time again, with a call to absolute obedience. The *key thought* being of course *Submission.*

In the general synopsis of the book we find 1) God's dealings with Israel in the past; 2) a repetition of the decalogue; 3) a new code of laws; 4) the real meaning of death and life; 5) Moses' final words and his song; and 6) his death and burial—and to this day no one knows the place where his body rests (Josh. 34, 6).

The *key word* of the book is *"remember."* This word is used repeatedly throughout the book. *"Remember"* 1) The Giving of the Law; 2) the new Covenant; 3) the Past Slavery; 4) The Great Deliverance; 5) the Divine Leadership; 6) The Sins of the Past; 7) Divine Judgment; 8) The ancient Days.

Notable passages: The Great Commandment; Remember God's Word; The Danger of Idolatry; The Blessings of Devotion to God and the curse and cause of sin.

We, too, can always use the word "Remember," especially when we "remember" how often Christ said, *"It is written";* and when He said, "Think not that I came to destroy the Law and the Prophets; I came not to destroy but to fulfill" (Matt. 5,17). Cf. Rom. 3, 31; Gal. 3,24.

Speaking of Christ, Moses said: "The Lord thy God will raise up unto thee a *prophet;* like unto me; unto Him ye shall hearken" (Deut. 18,15). "And," says Phillip to Nathanael, "we have found Him of whom Moses in the Law, and the Prophets did write,

Jesus of Nazareth; the son of Joseph" (John 1,45). Cf. Gen. 3,15; 49,10. And, Moses even calls Christ a *"prophet"* (Deut. 18,15). (Also "Star of Jacob") (Num. 24,27); "Seed of a Woman" (Gen. 3,15); "Sceptre of Israel" (Gen. 49,10); "Shiloh," literally, a prophetic name for Christ our Lord and Savior (Gen. 49,10).

In the days of Moses, too, people were converted, born anew, spiritually reborn (Num. 30, 6), which, by the act of regeneration, the soul, previously dead in sin, received spiritual life thorugh the workings of the Holy Spirit. The instrumental cause (if it may be called that) is God's Word, Old Testament as well as New Testament. The evidence is conviction of sin, genuine sorrow, deep humility, spiritual knowledge, faith a repentence, love and devotion to God's glory. Cf. Ps.103,3; Isa. 1, 16, 17, 25; 4, 4; 35, 5,6; 42,16; Jer. 24, 7, 9; Ezek. 18, 31; Zech. 12, 10.

Finally: regardless of what the efforts may be on the part of such as believe only what they can see, feel and experience, Moses nevertheless presents to us, not a report on social reform, racial integration and/or ethical information, but through all his writings he presents to us (seek and ye shall find) Christ on every page and Christ for every age.

The Book of Joshua

The Book of Joshua deals with the Israeli conquest and division of the Land of Canaan. The *key* thought being: *"How to Succeed in the Battle of Life"* (Josh. 1,8,9). Its historical analysis we might list as follows: 1) The invasion of the land; 2) the fall of Jericho; 3) then Ai, Ebad, and Gerizim; 4) the conquest of the south; 5) the listing of the dead kings; 6) a list of refuge cities; 7) Joshua's farewell address and death.

In the Book of Joshua, perhaps more than anywhere else, we find the certainty of the fulfillment of God's eternal promises and purposes, such as serious judgments pronounced because of the sins of the people; yet, God's *promise* is fulfilled to the descendants of Abraham "Unto thy seed will I give this land" (Gen. 12,17).

Typically, we might list these: The Canaanites, a type of our Spiritual enemies (Eph. 6,12); the warfare of Israel, a type of flight of faith (1 Tim. 6,12); Israel's rest after the final conquest, a type of the rest for the soul (Hebr. 4, 9); the Canaanites' party being subdued, a type of beseting sins, unconquered (Hebr. 12, 1).

In his farewell address Joshua refers to Abraham's "multiplied seed," and makes a new covenant with the people regarding his words as stated in the Book of the Law.

It is commonly understood that the crossing of the Jordan represents for us, death; and that Canaan represents heaven and all its glory.

The Book of Judges

The Book of Judges relates to six servitudes, civil wars, the period of confusion and anarchy; with special messages relative to Human Failure versus Divine Mercy and the deliverance of Israel. It also deals with the power of prayer, especially when the people *cried* repeatedly to God for pardon and peace. Compare now Paul's letter to the Galatians: "I marvel that ye are so soon removed from Him that called you unto the grace of Christ, unto another Gospel" (Gal. 1, 1-11); the backsliding of the Galatian church into sheer ceremonialism.

Speaking of The Gospel: there is only *one* gospel. And the people of the Old Testament were indeed saved by the same "gospel" as we have; they believed in the Messiah that *was to come* (Isa. 19, 20; 53, 8; Dan. 9, 25, 26); and we believe in the Messiah *that did come;* "For unto you is born this day in the city of David a Savior, which is Christ the Lord" (Luk. 2,11). Cf. Isa. 2, 2; 9, 6; Ps. 2, 2; 45, 7.

There are six parables listed in the Old Testament, so you see Christ was not alone with His many parables. I like parables, and I have written many in my day. Will you pardon me when I insert a short one herewith, as follows:

Laurie Anne, was her name, age, 17.

Angela, her mother, a noted neurologist, was a divorcee, the second time. Joakim Netherland, her dad, she had never seen.

From infancy Laurie was shuttled around between careless hired people, who, for the most part left her alone to take care of herself the best way she could; and thus, even as a teenager she became fully exposed to all the temptations and allurements of a most wicked and vicious world.

Then one day her mother got unexpected company, a police officer came to tell her that her daughter had been arrested and charged with prostitution (offering indiscriminate sexual intercourse in exchange for money).

When her mother then asked Laurie if this could possibly be true, Laurie answered: "Why not? You have done this for many years, only in a 'refined' manner. That's why you have had two husbands, yet none as of today."

Laurie Anne was a very beautiful girl, but very lonely. At night she would don herself up in enticing apparel and douse herself with fragrant perfumes; then repeatedly visit hotel and motel lobbies and men's waiting rooms with the idea that she might be invited to spend the night with them in bed. And it worked.

She never failed to accomplish that which was her purpose.

Laurie kept herself bodily clean and attractive; she knew how to avoid such nasty diseases as gonorrhea and syphilis; in other words, even at the age of only 17, she knew all the tricks of the trade.

And *why* was it possible that Laurie Anne could sink so low? To begin with she was both healthy and wealthy, beautiful and charming. What really was missing in her life?

First of all she lacked parenthood. She lacked companionship. Time and time again she had complained to her mother that she was not brought up like other girls in the neighborhood. Often she had asked her mother why they could not go to church like other people did, sing in the church choir, etc.

Laurie Anne was not a harlot or an iniquitous and corrupt person to begin with. She had become the victim of circumstances, *destroyed;* actually, by her own mother. She had been cheated and swindled out of everything good that rightly belonged to her, namely, the right and privilege to come in contact with God fearing people who would have given her full opportunity to share in a better life.

The question now is: what can we do for the thousands and thousands of other Laurie Annes with whom we come in contact every day?

Many of our young people today think the church is *too well organized*–too many rules, too much doctrine. And right here is where they can find an outlet for the extra "steam" that they have, if and when they are boiling over with enthusiasm, and wish to get out and do something real worthwhile on their own.

In fact this **should** be a real project for our young people, since they are in direct contact with this part of society, and they, better than anyone else, know what is going on in our local communities. And this they can do without getting their own feet wet.

So then, as soon as you "smell smoke" call the fire department (consult your own conscience); in other words, as soon as you see your own kind with whom you come in contact, get out of line, *call them back.*

Remind them that for the most part sensual desires and aspirations for the opposite sex are a normal behavior; *but;* that carnal sensuality (free indulgence in the gratification of the senses) is a most damnable sin; a sin against yourself, against your fellow-beings, and most of all against God, your Lord and Savior.

Remember too, that regardless of how far Laurie Anne has wandered away from her Lord; no matter how much she has hurt herself and others, *God still loves her* (John 8, 4-9).

So we say to all Laurie Annes: *Come back to Jesus;* He will never turn you away. Take His hand and let Him lead you on from now on. Trust Him. (Luk. 19,10; 1 Tit. 1,15; Hebr. 7,25).

The Book of Ruth

The Book of Ruth (a real literary *gem* if there ever was one) relates to a common cause of today, "equal rights for women." Here we have a *Gentile* woman that went so far as to actually become exalted to a *royal line;* and thus was made a member of the family of Christ, an ancestor of the Son of God; her son being the grandfather of David (Ruth 4,17). Cf. Matt 1,5,6.

Associated with her in character studies we find none other than Jephtha, Deborah, and Samson.

The book stresses as a spiritual message, 1) Human Failure; 2) The Power of Prayer; and concludes with a brief genealogy, from Pharez to Samuel.

First Book of Samuel

The book centers around three characters, 1) Samuel, the last of the Judges; 2) Saul, the first king of Israel; 3) David, Israel's most versatile king.

Some of the leading topics are, Samuel's remarkable boyhood; David slays the big giant, Goliath; the last years of Saul's reign, and his suicide.

The absolute rule of the Judges ends, the kingdom is established, and David, son of Jesse (see Jesse's *stem* in Isa. 11, 1, 11; Acts 13, 22, 23), becomes king (Chap. 16), himself a type and symbol of the Messiah.

Among its spiritual messages we find prayer was the dominating element in the life of Samuel. In fact he was born in answer to prayer (1 Sam. 10, 10-21); the name in itself means: "*Asked of God*" (1 Sam. 1,20).

But there was also in the life of Samuel divisions from the Divine Law, resulting in poligamy; parental indulgence; trust in sacred objects; impatience; and lack of obedience.

The Second Book of Samuel

The main subject in this book is the life of David, bad as well as good, and I know of no better way to list these than to quote my article from *Christian News;* dated March 15, 1976, to wit:

David was beautiful, courageous, charming, a great soldier and a man of war. However, in spite of his military policy his trend was towards the things that proceed from heaven (I Kings 15,5).

David was also a poet of renown; read first his psalms numbers 8, 19, and 23.

He was not only a king and poet but also a prophet; and he prophesied that "Christ's body would not be left in the grave" (Ps. 16,10); that "Christ was a Priest like Melchizedeck" (Ps. 110,4); that "Christ would be betrayed by a familiar friend" (Ps. 41,9); that "the office who betrayed Christ would be filled by another" (Ps. 109, 8); that "false witnesses would accuse Him" (Ps. 27,12); that "He would be hated without cause" (Ps. 69,4); that "while on the cross He would be offered gall and vinegar" (Ps. 69,21); that "He would be hated without cause" (Ps. 69,4); that "while on the cross He would be mocked and insulted" (Ps. 22, 6-8); that "He would have to listen to His own "prophetic words repeated in mockery" (Ps. 22,8); that His legs would not be broken while on the cross in order to hasten his death" (Ps. 53,9); that "the soldiers would cast lots for His coat" (Ps.22,18); that

"He would rise again from the grave" (Ps. 16,10); that "He would finally go home to His father in heaven" (Ps. 68,18); that "in spite of all this He would still keep on praying for His enemies" (Ps. 109, 4)!

There were of course times when David was led astray by extreme passion, love of money and power and lust for women (Deut. 17, 17; 2 Sam. 5, 13); when he yielded to gross sins (2 Sam. Chapter 11). He was severely rebuked by Nathan, the prophet, with whom he confered on the building of the Temple (2 Sam. 7, 1-7). However, scripturewise, David was charged with only *one* sin (1 Kings 15,4,5).

Humanly speaking David was just another person like you and me, who in God's sight sinned every day, in thought, word and deed. For his sorrow over his sins and his feeling of guilt and his voluntary admission of culpability, please read his fifty-first psalm. Cf. Psalm 6,6; 40, 6; wherein he confesses his sin and throws himself wholly over to God's love and mercy (Ps. 58,3).

No human being illustrates more fully the moral range and way off distance to which behavior and conduct can lead us than does David's life as a whole. When I think of David I at once begin to wonder that there can be so much actual good in others, and yet so much utter filth and damnation in my own flesh!

With this thought in mind David becomes, to me, a prince of virtue and a mountain peak among all human beings.

Therefore, through him, the royal line was established, and through him it will continue through Solomon, his son, and on through Judah, forever.

In his youth David was an athlete (1 Sam. 34-36). He also was a fine musician, even to the extent that he played before the king (1 Sam. 16,14-23). His poetic genius was of the highest possible order, and he wrote some of the greatest masterpieces of spiritual literature the world has ever had. A large number of the psalms are accredited to him, and have been constantly used by the Church throughout all ages.

He was an able general, and conducted his military campaigns with huge success.

David was born at Bethlehem, where he spent his childhood,

and grew up on his father's fields; he was the youngest of his father's eight sons ("Jesse's" son—Ruth 4, 22).

He was but a youth when summoned to Saul's court to assist in the soothing over the bemuddled mind of the king, by playing his harp for him (1 Sam. 16, 23).

GOLIATH THE GREAT

The Israelites and the Philistines stand ready for battle, and David now challenges Goliath the huge champion; the large and gigantic hero of the Philistines. They all made fun of David, of course, the little kid from the sheepyard. But David was not scared in the least, because he knew that the Lord was on his side. Besides, had he not just recently also killed both a lion and a bear with his own hands while they sought to carry away his helpless lambs?

There were some of his own people that tried to talk him out of tackling Goliath, but finally they said: "Go, the Lord be with you."

Then Saul dressed David up in full armour, with five little pebbles in his bag and a slingshot in his hand. As the terrible-looking monster saw David come he called him a dog, cursed him and said: "Come right on you silly little boy, and I will see to it that your carcass becomes a feast for the birds and beasts."

So David placed a pebble in his slingshot, took good aim, swung, let go, and the pebble came with such force that it sank deep into Goliath's forehead; and Goliath fell forward on his face to the ground, after which David put his foot on his body, took Goliath's sword and cut off his head.

Then all the Philistines fled, and David took Goliath's head with him to Jerusalem (1 Sam. 17, 1-58).

Soon after his masterful victory over Goliath, David was made military commander, and later married Michal (1 Sam. 18, 27-29), the king's youngest daughter, to whom David was devotedly attached. Saul canceled the marriage and gave Michal to Phalti, a native of Gallim. David later reclaimed Michal, but the union was not a success.

The extraordinary events in the life of David were: 1) The execution of the Amalekites; and his intense sorrow over Saul and Jonathan; 2) the great battle between the followers of David and the servants of Ishbosheth, who was killed after a reign of two short years; 3) David's special obedience to God's command and guidance; 4) his severe punishment of those who tried to bribe him; 5) by his realization of the fact that his exaltation to the throne was an act of God; 6) that all his conquests were due to God's Power.

DAVID'S FALL AND PUNISHMENT

"Lord, lead us not into temptation!" But David just forgot to say his prayers that night; and when nightfall came he amused himself by watching a beautiful, naked, married woman, take her bath (2 Sam. 11, 2); her name was Bathsheba.

David's sexual desires ran aloof; and his next move was to see to it that he get this woman for his own; but that was no problem for David, since Bathsheba's husband, Uriah, was an officer of high rank in David's army, and it was easy for David to get him killed, "accidentally," which he did (2 Sam. 12-9; 23, 30).

Was Bathsheba ever charged as an accomplice in this dastardly act of David's? No, she was not; on the contrary she "mourned for her husband" (2 Sam. 11, 26) and she subsequently also pleaded for Adonijah, David's son, although he deceived her (1 Kings 2,13-15). Later Bathsheba loved David, married him, became pregnant, and became the mother of Solomon, through David (2 Sam. 12, 24; 5, 13,14).

By this marriage Bathsheba indirectly becomes a member of the family of our Lord and Savior, and counted worthy of being listed as an ancestor of Christ (Matt. 1, 6). In this connection let us not forget that there are two other women also listed as ancestors of Christ, Rahab, the harlot (Matt. 1,5); and Ruth; one very "bad," the other very good.

But all ended up well with Rahab, as it did with David for his wrong. She received and concealed Joshua's spies (by faith) in their exploration of Canaan (Josh. 2, 1-24), an act that saved her life; and what's more, Rahab was saved by faith (Hebr. 11, 31), and "perished not with them that *believed* not." And she was "justified by works" (James 2, 25), in like manner as was Abraham *the friend of God;* because he believed.

With all this in mind we MUST NOT FORGET that there is nothing in God's entire system of salvation outside of sin and grace, repentance and forgiveness, *Law and Gospel!* If and when we base our hope eternal on this one fact, then we may rest assured that we need no other religion of any kind.

THEN BACK TO DAVID ONCE AGAIN

When David confessed his sin, and forgiveness *in the same verse* one might think that God permitted David to get by with a "short cut" within the plans of God's eternal provisions. *No way.* Without sin there is no grace; without repentance there is no forgiveness; without Law there is no Gospel. And David knew this *very well.* That's *why* he said: "In sin did my mother conceive me" (Ps. 51, 5); "the wicked go estranged from the womb, they go astray as soon as they be born, speaking lies" (Ps. 58, 3). There was *no* "short cut" for David. There is *only* one way to heaven, and David knew this full well, since he helped give us the Scriptures in the first place.

Many a night he often wet his pillow with tears of sorrow (Ps. 6; 6). See also Ps. 32, 5; Ps. 38, 17: "My sorrow is continually before me." "I am poor and sorrowful" (Ps. 69,29); "I will be sorry for my sin" (Ps. 38, 18); "I will say unto God my Rock, Why hast Thou forgotten me?" (Ps. 42, 9); "I go mourning all day long" (Ps. 38, 6); "Hath God forgotten to be gracious?" "Hath His anger shut up His tender mercies?" (Ps. 77,9).

But David also knew about grace, about forgiveness; and he knew all about the Gospel too: "But there is forgiveness with Thee, that Thou mayest be feared" (Ps. 130, 4). "Why boastest thou thyself in mischief, O mighty man? the goodness of God *endureth* continually" (Ps. 52, 1). "They shall abundantly utter the memory of Thy great goodness, and shall sing of Thy righteousness" (Ps. 145,7). "Oh how great is Thy goodness, which Thou hast laid up for them that fear Thee; which Thou hast wrought for them that trust in Thee before the sons of men!" (Ps. 31,19); "I had fainted, unless I had believed to see the goodness of the Lord in the land of the living" (Ps. 27,13); "Surely goodness and mercy shall follow me all the days of my life; and I will dwell in the house of the LORD forever" (Ps. 23,6).

DAVID'S KINFOLKS

What a mess; corruption plus.

David's oldest son, Amnon (by his wife Ahinoan), raped his own sister, then threw her away like a wet rag (2 Sam. 13,1-21). Later, while he was drunk, Amnon was killed by Absalom's servants (ch. 13,28,29).

Then David's third son, Absalom, a beautiful person with gorgeous hair, who gained favor among the people, rebelled against his own father. But though he had a tremendous army, and well organized, he still was utterly defeated (2 Sam. 15,4; to 17, 24) when 20,000 men were slain. Defeated by his own father.

Then when Absalom came riding on a mule, and the mule went under a large oak, his beautiful hair got snarled in the limb of the tree; while he was still there hanging in mid air, while the mule walked away, Joah, (a son of Zeruiah, a sister of David) a generalissimo in David's army and an accomplished warrior and unscrupulous, took three darts in his hand and thrust them through Absalom's heart, while he was yet alive and hanging from the oak.

And this was done even though David had given strict orders that his son should be spared.

Then they took Absalom's body and threw it into a deep hollow in the ground, and covered it over with a great heap of stones (ch. 18,1-17).

And David was much moved; and he went up to the chamber over the gate, and wept; and as he went there he said: "My son, Absalom, my son, my son!

"Would God I had died for thee" (ch. 18, 23).

A worthless man by the name, Sheba, a Benjaminite, started an insurrection against David, and took many of David's men with him; but the men of Judah stayed with the king all the way to Jerusalem.

In Jerusalem David took the ten concubines he had left to keep the palace and put them in confinement, provided them with food, but had no intercourse with them. So they lived there like widows in confinement till he died (2 Sam. 20,1-3).

I mention some of these things to show that 1) there is a nasty ghost in every closet—something wrong in every home and family.

Christ's disciples did not always get along too well together either; and Judas Iscariot, after being with our Lord during His entire public ministry, betrayed his Master, for money; then hanged himself (Matt. 27,5), falling down headlong, he burst asunder in the midst, and all his bowels gushed out (Acts 1,18).

2) That if and when we write history we must *tell it as it is*. Even Christ Himself used hard words at times when he told the truth, and sin is not too easy to describe, because sin is sin!

Finally, the more we study the great men of the Scriptures, the more we find that David was, indeed, the grandest and most brilliant character in the entire history of man! No deed of human intrepidity has ever surpassed his encounter with the Philistine giant; no story of personal affection is more touching than that of the friendship between David and Jonathan; and one of the most pathetic scenes in the Bible is that of David's grief over Absalom.

No poems have ever so powerfully and profoundly appealed to the hearts and souls of men as have his psalms.

Notwithstanding all his faults and shortcomings, *David is*, in fact, forever, the type and symbol of the *Messiah;* our Lord and Savior, Jesus the Christ!

First Book of Kings

Now that David was dead, his own son Solomon becomes king. We read about the great splendor of his court and palaces (4, 22-

28); and about his fair judgment and surprising wisdom (4, 29-34; 7, 1-12); about the building of the Great Temple (5, 6); and about his great wealth (9, 17-23; 10, 14-29).

Then the other side of the coin: We also learn about the *decline* of his kingdom because of his extravagant luxury (10, 14-19); about his turning *away* from God (11, 4-8) and about the enemies that God stirred up against him (11, 14-20).

And Solomon dies (1 Kings 11,41), after which his son Rehoboam takes over the kingdom (11, 43; 12, 19).

The book also relates to the two Great Prophets, Elijah, and Elisha, relative to their miracles and missions (Chapters 17,18, 19 and 21). There will be a fuller detail of these in Second Kings.

Second Book of Kings

This book is a sequel to First Kings, and shows the power and influence a ruler has upon a nation, especially when a spiritual message is involved. The first part of the book has a great deal to say about the Prophet Elijah.

Elijah (as was also the case with Elisha) left no writings. He appears as *The Great;* and the most dramatic and unique character in Bible history, and he was a great reformer, too. In several instances God honored him with very extraordinary miraculous power.

Another very special thing about Elijah is that God exempted him from ordinary death and transported him to heaven by special means (2, 2-11).

Then the Prophet Elisha (left no writings) was specially rewarded by God because he asked for a *double* portion of His grace and mercy (2,9). Elisha performed twelve of the greatest miracles recorded in the Scriptures (Chapters, 2, 3, 4 and 5); and effected eight other matters manifesting unusual power (Chapters 6 and 13).

The secret of his power was that he depended wholly on

God's Divine Power, favor, and assurance; and upon that framework of procedure he acted within the spirit of victory!

In many cases his multiple miracles remind us of the many great miracles Christ performed. No prophet was more like unto Christ than was Elisha. His gentility and refinement gained for him a position in life so strong that the troubled waters and stormy seas became his effective and desired result.

Perhaps the most spectacular thing about the life of Elisha was that he actually appeared together with Moses *talking* to Jesus during His transfiguration (Matt. 17, 1-3; Mk. 9, 4; Luk, 28, 30).

And, was not Elisha also the forerunner of John the Baptist (Matt. 11, 14); Luk. 1,17), who in turn was the forerunner of Christ? (Mal. 3, 1; Isa. 40, 3; Luk. 1, 7).

How much closer can you tie Christ into the Old Testament than this?

First and last, always: that's *Christ;* everywhere, now and forever.

First Book of Chronicles

This book is a supplement to The First Book of Kings. The central character being *David;* as has often been said before, one of the most promiment figures in the world, for Jew, Gentile and Christians alike; a mountain peak among Bible characters and the most famous among the ancestors of Christ.

In fact Jesus is not called the Son of Abraham, nor the Son of Jacob, but He *is* called, seven times, *The Son of David* (Matt. 9,27;21,9; Mk. 10,47,48; 15,22; Luk. 18,38,39)!

The Second Book of Chronicles

This book is largely supplemental and deals with Solomon's building of the Temple, and the reign of Solomon; the folly of Rehoboam; the power of prayer brings victory, and the glory of God fills the Temple.

The Book of Ezra

Ezra, the Scribe, who honored God's Word by *searching* it; by publicly reading and exposing it (Neh. 8, 2-8; Ezra 7,11).

He calls for the inauguration of social and religious reform; sets forth the Power of God's Word in human life; and expounds The Law of Moses (3,2); and the Commandments (6, 14; 10, 3-5), and the Law of God (7, 10-14).

Ezra was associated with Nehemiah in initiating a revival of the study of the Scriptures (Neh. Chapter 8) and to have assembled most of the books of the Old Testament.

He is the reputed author of many of the Psalms, notably the 119th Psalm, which contains 168 references (verses) to rules, tenets, commandments, laws, etc.

Everywhere we turn in the Old Testament we come in direct contact with the Law and the prophets. It was to these to whom Christ always turned when troubled by His enemies (Matt. 5, 17; Rom. 3,31; Gal. 3,24).

The Book of Nehemiah

Nehemiah was the fifth Leader of Israel and during his time he made two trips to Jerusalem. Many Bible scholars regard his book more or less an autobiography.

He overcame the ridicule, greed, contempt and rebuke of his friends by hard work, self-sacrificing example, steadfast courage and confession of God's goodness and watchful prayer.

His last words were: *"Remember* me O God, for good" (Neh. 13,31).

The Book of Esther

Here is one book in which the name of God does not appear at all, and, in which the name of (Ahasuerus) a heathen king is referred to more than a hundred times! With the exception of fasting, the book contains no mention of prayer or spiritual services of any kind.

The only reason that this book has been accepted as being *inspired* and given a place in Holy Writ is the fact that King Ahasuerus advanced Esther to become queen, and, at her request, delivered the Jews (God's people) from the utter destruction and complete extermination planned by Haman, who himself eventually was hanged upon the very gallows he had built for the hanging of Mordecai, uncle of the queen.

And thus the two-day Feast of Purim was instituted, and is celebrated by the Jews to this very day (Est. 9, 26, 27).

In speaking of the Old Testament Kings, let us remember *this;* that of the nineteen kings of Israel (Jeroboam (I) to Hosken) they were *all* men of the lowest possible type; and, of the twenty kings of Judah (Jeroboam (I) to Jasiah), of the 20, *only five* were men of good character.

Take for instance *Ahab;* that weak-minded, idolatrous wicked tool of an ungodly wife. Please read on, as follows:

Ahab was the son of Omri, and the seventh king of Israel.

He lived in Jezeel, Issacher, a city which he had beautified with ornamental buildings and an ivory house.

Through the influence of his passionate and ambitious idolatrous wife, the worship of Baal and Ashtorath was introduced in

Israel, and the prophets of God were haunted, persecuted and killed.

Ahab was notoriously wicked, and continued with his blasphemous life to the extent that God sent Elijah to pronounce judgment upon him and all his descendants (1 Kings 21, 22). Cf. Micah, 1 Kings 22, 28.

GOD IS NOT MOCKED

Ahab's wife, Jezebel, in the course of time, was thrown out (down) of the window, and some of her blood splattered on the horses and the wall, and she was trampled on.

When the day came to bury her they found only her skull, her feet, and the palms of her hands; the dogs had had their day, as had been predicted.

Jehu had told them what Elijah had said, namely, that dogs would devour Jezebel's body, and that her flesh would be like manure on the ground; all of which came true in accordance with what Elijah had said.

All of Ahab's seventy sons were beheaded, their heads brought in a basket and piled up at the city gate. In fact all of Ahab's friends and relatives were killed in the battle at Ramothgilead, where Ahab also was killed, the dogs licking up his blood while his servants were washing his chariot, a partial fulfillment of Elijah's predictions (1 Kings 21,19; 22,38).

In 1951 I visited with Richard Nixon here. I was also present and visited with him again at the inauguration of President Eisenhower in 1953. I still have his official 13 x 18 portrait in oil hanging in my office, as well as a keepsake letter he wrote me on my 90th birthday in 1971.

Ahab was a king and ruler in his day, as was also President Richard Nixon. They both failed, utterly.

What was it, really, that made them turn to the left instead of turning to the right? Sin, of course! Power, prestige and love of money.

The word "prestige" comes to us from the French, and means, literally, a *blindfolding;* or, to be misled.

King Herod Agrippa, for instance, persecuted the apostles, beheaded James, and tried to execute Peter (Acts 12, 1-21).

So then, percentage-wise, Richard Nixon did not fare too bad. It might have been worse. But even as of this day I am not too sure that Nixon ever has repented of his wickedness. If he has not, his ultimate fate is very bad, indeed.

Take a tip from: "THE OLD MAN ON THE CORNER," and keep your nose out of dirty politics; and as soon as you have too much money, *get rid of it; and fast!*

The Book of Job

Many scholars regard the Book of Job as being the oldest book in the Bible. It is both poetical and pictorial, but deals mainly with the problem of Job's afflictions.

It shows Job first as a godly father, unspoiled by prosperity, ministering as a priest to a large family (1, 5).

Then Satan enters, trying to sell Job on the idea that he serves God for services received (1, 9-11).

Time and time again Satan enters and reenters, and, almost wins, until God says, "That's enough for now"; and God rewards Job double (42, 10).

In the Book of Job we learn two things, first the malignant power of the devil in our own personal lives; second, as Christ so often has taught us, that it takes strong acid to remove rust and stains, and, that the use of trials and tribulations is the *Divine Plan* leading us to perfected faith in the merits of Christ our Lord (Acts 14, 22; Rom. 12, 12; 8, 35).

The final scene in the life of Job is that he calls Jesus Christ his *Redeemer* (19, 25). Cf. Ps. 19, 14; Prov. 23, 11; Jer. 50,34. Also: "Prince of the princes" (8, 25) and "Messiah the Prince" (9,25) and "Messiah" (9,26).

The Psalms

This book contains one hundred and fifty spiritual songs and poems used by the Church of all ages in worship and devotional exercises. It was used as the hymn book of the Second Temple.

The predominant themes are of course prayer and praise, but the psalms also cover a great variety of religious and personal experiences. They are quoted more frequently then any other book in the Bible, with the exception of the Book of Isaiah.

David composed most of the psalms, but others did too, for instance the sons of Korah, Asaph, Heman, Ethan, Solomon, Moses, Haggie, Zechariah, Hezekiah and Ezra, and some who remain anonymous.

Christ is often referred to in the Psalms: "And *He* said unto them, "these are the words which I spake unto you, while I was yet with you that all things must be fulfilled which were written in the Law of Moses, and in the Psalms concerning Me", (Luk. 24,44; 20,18; Mk. 8, 31; 9, 22, 12,10; 18,31).

Then too the Psalms are replete with *Messianic* announcements (sixty-three at least); and no less than thirty-five statements about Christ (in the Psalms) are referred back to in the New Testament, relating to Christ's Advent; His mission; to the treatment He did receive (or was to) receive; to His Betrayal; to His Death and His Crucifixion, etc.

In Psalms twenty-two there is scarcely a single line that does not in some manner connect with our Lord; and *every part* of Psalm One Hundred Ten applies to Christ.

In this book we also find some very special names applied to Christ: "King of Glory" (24,7,10); "Man of God's Right Hand" (80,17). Cf. also Ps. 2,2; 45, 3,3; 89,27. And still some people say we do not need the Old Testament.

The Book of Proverbs

In Norwegian we call this book: *Solomon's Ordsprog;* that is, Solomon's sayings. The book contains instructions concerning right living; also brief discourses relative to Wisdom, Justice, Temperance, Industry, Purity of Life, etc.

In his most vigorous and sometimes sarcastic sayings, a sharp contrast is drawn between Wisdom and Folly, between Righteousness and Sin; between that which is Good and that which is Evil. It's a great book for young people.

It tells us what makes an ideal wife, and warns against evil women.

"*Every Word* of God is Pure; He is a Shield unto them that put their trust in Him. *Add thou not unto his word;* lest He reprove thee, and thou be found a liar" (Prov. 30,5,6). Cf. Deut. 4,2; Rev. 22,18.

I wonder sometimes if the words in the foregoing do not apply directly to the conditions in our Church today!

The Book of Ecclesiastes

This book has often been refered to as the "Preacher's Book." It was most likely also written by Solomon. It deals with the search of natural man for satisfaction and happiness; and, that these are not found in the acquisition of either wisdom, wordly pleasure, agriculture, great possessions, epicureanism, or materialism (Chaps. 1 and 2).

The conclusions are that vanity of riches, eat and drink create vexation of God's Spirit and disregard of religious duties, and ends up with God's judgment (Chaps. 10 to 16).

And these are the *Laws* to which Christ appealed *so often* while still with us (Acts 26, 22).

As soon as we mention "The Preacher's Book," we at once begin to think specially of *doctrine*. Christ was "great" on doctrine, and whether He spoke in parables or performed miracles or just taught and/or preached, it all had to do with one thing: *Law and Gospel;* and that *one thing* was that there was only *one way* to life eternal, and that was *through Him* (John 14,6). Cf. John 1,17; 8,32. Even Moses was firm on doctrine (Deut. 32, 2) "So shall *my word* be that goeth forth out of *My* mouth; it shall not return unto Me void" (Isa. 56,11). Cf. Isa. 28,9.

If we examine closely Christ's teachings we will find that there is perhaps not a single Christian Doctrine that He did not touch on, as for instance, marriage, civil government, conscience, heaven, hell, immortality, sin, grace, repentance, justification, sanctification, faith, predestination, etc., etc.

It is hard for us to believe and to understand that the entire work of sanctification, namely, that by the Gospel the Holy Ghost has *called* us, enlightened, justified, sanctified us, and *will keep us in faith to the end;* and, that all this was *not by chance;* but that God resolved all this for you and for me long before the world began.

Of course we have no advance knowledge of our election unto life eternal, but we *know by the results* in our lives, by faith that "No man shall ever pluck us out of God's hand" (John 10, 29). Cf. John 14,28. So, with your kind permission I present for you a short elucidation of the doctrine of Predestination, to wit:

What Does Predestination Really Mean?

The doctrine of Predestination (more correctly called *The Election to Grace*) is the work of the Holy Ghost, by which we are brought to Christ through the Gospel ("called" by the Gospel) and thus assured that by grace through faith, we are converted, justifed, and will be kept in faith until our salvation is completed in the glory of heaven.

Our Predestination is not a matter of chance, since God had planned it all carefully, resolved it and designed it especially, but just for that (some) special person, that particular person, in order to bring that person (you and I) to the Gospel of Christ.

All this He had done (decreed and ordained) for you and for me, long before time began, not according to our works, but according to His grace (2 Tim. 1,9; Eph. 1,36; Acts 13,49).

Predestination does not pertain to the redemption by which salvation was obtained for *all* men; nor to the means of grace through which the spiritual blessings were to be imparted to men, but it pertains to *man;* Man *himself;* namely, to that *particular person;* you and me, as individuals, to *us* (Eph. 1,4); to *you* (2 Thes. 2,13).

HOW AM I TO KNOW THAT I HAVE BEEN ELECTED?

God has not, in so many words, specifically revealed to us *who* the elect are. But we may rest assured that by searching God's Word we will soon recognize ourselves as among God's chosen ones by the *results* of our election, that is, by the lives we are living, and, as for instance, by our conversion, by our repentance, by our sins being forgiven, by a continued sanctified life and good works, and, by the assurance that a glorified heaven awaits us!

Further than this *scripture sayeth not;* except that God *did* choose us, select us, preferred us, actually *picked us out* of the many others; also that He did *not* extend this election to all people, but only to "few" (Matt. 22,14).

All this He did—decreed, and planned long before we were born, and by this *He made us his own* (John 10,14), all of which makes our election *sure;* so *sure* that nothing will ever pluck us out of God's hand (John 10,28).

Still you say: But how can I believe that God's *choice of me is a reality?* Surely, you believe God's concern for you to the extent that you have eternal life through faith (John 3, 16)? Then, by the same token you must also believe that God's love for you and His concern for you extends to the point whereby he *did* ordain and elect you to eternal life (Acts 13,48). See also Acts 2, 47.

By faith we not only believe but we *know*; and a Scriptural knowledge of our election increases our confidence in our ultimate salvation and assures us that our joy in heaven will be most extraordinary, indeed! It would be a great sin on our part to further speculate concerning the unlimited and undeniable foreknowledge of God. Rather than this, we should repent of our daily sins, hear the Gospel of Grace and *believe*. If we have faith in the Gospel, we will also have to acknowledge that the Gospel of Grace and our election to salvation go hand in hand, and that we cannot have the one without the other.

The Gospel itself is what brings us the great news that our election begins and ends within the realms of God's grace, and thus brings us a victory that can end only in union with the Holy Trinity (2 Thes. 2,13; Eph. 1,4;1 Pet. 1,2).

WHY JUST A FEW, WHY JUST A FEW?

Nowhere does Scripture teach that there is a Predestination unto damnation (for all who are lost). Scripture, though *does* teach that God most seriously and firmly declares that He would have *all men come to the knowledge of the truth;* and be saved. So we must conclude that those who are lost are lost because they did not wish to come to the knowledge of the truth, but avoided and (at least inwardly) rejected the call of God's Spirit; and the fact that they *are lost* in their own fault.

Holy Writ makes no attempt to explain to us the apparent discrepancy that exists between the doctrine of universal grace and the doctrine of election to salvation by grace and grace alone. This, too, is a matter that our improverished mind cannot understand.

So then, let's not put God up against a test tube, nor attempt to pry into His eternal resolutions!

As before herein stated, God knows of no such arrangement but firmly wishes that *all* men be saved (1 Tim. 2,4), and that man and man alone is at fault if and when he is lost (Matt 23,37). See also Hos. 13,9.

Synergism (means a working together) teaches that God begins and man completes; that God makes conversion a possibility, but man makes it a reality. So, they say, there *must* be something in man that influences and affects God to elect just some (not many) and not the others.

But Scripture says, most emphatically, that there is no element or component of human merit in faith, and thus denies that there is any worthiness or excellence on our part that could be a cause or reason for Him to elect us to eternal life (2 Tim. 1,9).

As stated before; That God by grace for Christ's sake will have all men to be saved, and, that God, by grace, for Christ's sake, also elected a small number to be saved, human reason cannot understand, nor must we try to do so. This mystery God has reserved for Himself and Himself alone. Let's leave well enough alone!

The Songs of Solomon

This book, highly dramatic in love, has been severely criticized because of its "sexy" and amorous language.

Its proper place in the Scriptures, however, has been defended by serious-minded scholars, as well as men of mature mind of all ages, who regard these love stories as spiritual allegories and a symbolical narration representing the Holy affections existing between God and His chosen people, or between Christ and His Church.

For instance: A spiritual communion between the Bride and the Heavenly Bridegroom. The Bride is lonesome for her companion and tries to find him. The ardent discourse of the Bride and the Bridegroom on their mutual love and the graces of each other.

We, as believers, call Christ "Our Beloved" (2, 16). Cf. Ps. 45.

The Bridegroom's (Christ's) love covers all defects of the Bride (4, 7); He rejoices over Her (Isa. 62,5); He gave His life for her (Eph. 5,25); He will come and claim Her as His own (Matt.

25,6); the Bride LOVES the Bridegroom (SS 2,16); He feels Her unworthiness (SS 1,5); the Bride (the Church)—you and I—have been purified and dressed in spotless robes (Rev. 19,8); the Bride wears the jewels of Divine grace (Isa. 61,10); and the purified Church sends out the invitations to the wedding (Rev. 22,17).

And then comes the grand wedding supper: prepared by the Father and the Son (Matt. 22,2); the costly preparations are made (Matt. 22,4); the invitations to the great honor (Rev. 19,9); but these sacred invitations are scorned by the multitudes (Matt. 22,5); in spite of them being sent to all classes of people (Matt. 22,10) all who come or try to come to this grand wedding party will not be allowed to enter, because they are not clad in the garments required (Matt. 22,11-13).

We do love him (indeed, we, the Church, too) *do* love Him (2,16), though we also *do feel* our great unworthiness (1,5); but through faith in His suffering, His death, and His Resurrection we become dressed in the robe of Righteousness gained for us by the Bride (Christ), Rev.10,8; and our Church (and we) will forever wear the jewels of Divine Grace (Isa. 61,10); that is, *if* our Church remains true to the Law and the Gospel (The Law and the prophets) in the manner Christ commanded: *"All things that He commanded"* (Matt. 28,20), and not teach just a social gospel based on friendly conversations and good companionship. Cf. Rom. 12,7; Col. 1, 28; Tit. 1,11.

The Book Isaiah

Many of the passages in the Book of Isaiah are among the finest in all literature. Nevertheless, it has been and still is greatly misunderstood and misinterpreted. Some people, especially the "learned" ones, study the book in about the same manner as a gardener would study his flowers. First they go about it in a manner so lethargic that by the time they get through picking it apart there is nothing left except the wilted and lifeless stem.

One of the first things Isaiah does is to foretell the coming of Christ's Kingdom, exhorting his people to fear because of the powerful effects of God's majesty.

He writes about the sins and misery of his people, but promises salvation in his "Song of Confidence" in God.

The second part of the book contains predictions, warnings, and promises which refer to events beyond the captivity, and reach on down through the centuries and past the Christian dispensation.

This portion of the book is prophetically and specially rich in Messianic references. (Points us to Christ over and over again!)

Isaiah refers to Christ, not only as being gentle (42, 3) but also as a Law-giver (11, 4), not only as a Prince of Peace (9,6) but also as a judge (11, 3), not only as being meek (53,7) but also as a reprover (11,4), etc. Then he goes on depicting our Lord and Savior as being "The King," eight times, as being the "Son of David," seven times, and honoring him with titles like "The Intervener" (53, 12), "The Liberator" (42,7), "The Burden-bearer" (53,4) "Immanuel" (7,14), "Mighty God" (9,6), "Everlasting Father" (9,6), "Prince of Peace" (9,6), "OUR Only Savior" (53,5), etc. in fact eighty titles in all. Read specially Isaiah, Chapter 53!

In his Messianic Prophecies Isaiah looks down into the forthcoming centuries with a clear eye on the Son of God, Jesus Christ our Lord and Savior.

In this he has given us a most perfect picture of the history, mission, titles, and characteristics of Christ.

The Book of Jeremiah

Jeremiah, The Weeping Prophet, rejected by his neighbors, deserted by his own family, cast off by priests and prophets alike, rebuffed by his friends, abandoned by his people at large, discarded and forsaken by the King—no wonder he wept!

Once he was smitten and put in stocks (20,2); once he was

cast into a dungeon where he sank into the mud (8,6).

But Jeremiah nevertheless continued to denounce the rulers and the evil work of False Prophets and False Shepherds and their mutilations of God's Word.

He predicted persecution and Divine Judgment and the overthrow of Jerusalem, and foretold the Seventy Years of Captivity (25,29); but on the other hand he also held out hope for the people and the restoration of the Jews (30, 30).

Through it all he was sustained and comforted by the Word of God (15,16). And, might we close with his final words: "In his days Judah shall be saved, and Israel shall dwell safely; and this is His name whereby He shall be called, *The Lord Our Righteousness*'" (Jer.23,6; 33,16). "Son of man" [CHRIST] Ezek.2,1. Cf. Matt. 24,27.

"The Voice of Joy, and the Voice of Gladness, the Voice of the Bridegroom, and the Voice of the Bride, and of them that shall say: Praise the Lord, for His mercy endureth forever" (33, 16).

Who was it that said that Christ was not to be found in the Old Testament?

Then too, Jeremiah calls Christ "The Lord of Righteousness" (Jer, 23,6;33,16); and Christ is promised (Jer. 31,22).

The Book of Lamentations

This is a sequel to the Book of Jeremiah. It is written as though it were for a funeral of the Nation, portraying the capture and destruction of Jerusalem.

a) The book deals in general with the ruin of Jerusalem and the utter misery of the exiles, all because of their sins (Chap. 1). b) Jehovah, the ancient Defender of all Israel, has given up His people to bask in the mire of their own wickedness (Chap. 2). c) Jeremiah's grief over the afflictions of his own people— nevertheless, also, his absolute TRUST in God (Chap. 3). d) The former glory and happiness of Israel contrasted with their present misery and shame (Chap. 4). e) A prayer to God for His mercy and goodness (Chap. 5).

"Then sayeth the Lord unto me; Thou hast well seen; for I will hasten my Word to perform it" (1,12). So we again understand that *God is not mocked;* even though His Mercy endureth forever (Law and Gospel in one single sentence). Just what Christ came to preach.

Following the words of the "Weeping Prophet", might we now consider the fate of Carvo Lutchia and his wife Petronelia (in Parable) to wit:

Carvo Lutchia worked in a coal mine. Every night he came home from work dirty, tired and grouchy.

His wife Petranelia worked in a beer joint.

They had two children, Dora, age 15 (who smoked grass), and Archie, age 12, who lived for the most part in the streets.

There always was some food in the house, but no one to prepare it.

The house was never kept in order, and no hot water in which to wash clothes.

No one ever went to church or Sunday School, and there was no hymnal nor Bible in the home, and instead of sacred lyrics they turned to jazz and rock.

Then one day Archie ran away from home, "for good." At least that is what he said in his parting note.

Several months later police found a boy's bicycle on the bank of a far-away river, with the name "Archie" stamped on the handlebars. Many hours of dragging the river bottom with a grapel net brought no results, and finally the boy was considered lost.

Years went by. Archie's father had passed away, the funeral being conducted by the county authorities.

Dora was married, also to a coal miner; and they had three children, but no church and no Sunday School.

Archie's mother by this time was getting old and gray— hopeless and despondent, but still waiting and believing that Archie, her lost son, would some day come home.

Every night she would sing: "Archie, dear Archie, my darling; won't you please come home, come home!"

But Archie did not come home.

Then one day a middle-aged man by the name Lum Hing, employed by the Chuen Bible Society, called on Dora and her family. He was trying to make a little money so that he could get to attend the seminary. The book that he was selling was called: *Great News for All People*.

Lum Hing also left a little tract called: "Go Tell." It told all about Jesus, who He was, where He came from, where He finally went, and, that some day He is coming back.

Dora did not recognize her brother Archie, but Archie *did* recognize her; and then he told her who he was, and what had happened to him.

And here is what he told her: Archie had stepped on a loose rock as he left his bicycle on the river bank, falling headlong into the river. He was carried many miles down the rushing waters, and was finally dashed over the stony rapids and was knocked senseless, and completely lost his memory. He did not know who he was nor where he was.

It was then that a Christian Chinese family by the name of Ootzo Me found him and nursed him back to health and happiness, with a mind as good as ever. (So much for Archie.)

Dora's children were now enrolled in Sunday School; and there is just one thing missing—did Archie's parents ever get to know their Lord and Saviour?

This question may be answered by asking another question: Are we today doing what we should do in bringing the Law and the Gospel to the many millions who yet have never heard a single word about what happened on Good Friday 2000 years ago?

When you go to bed tonight, think about that!

The Book of Ezekiel

Like the Book of Daniel and the Book of Revelation, the Book of Ezekiel too might well be called a book of mystery. It is rich in imagery and picture writing. However, it also contains much that is very clear and of the highest possible importance.

Ezekiel claims for himself the loftiest degree of inspiration. The words: "Thus saith Jehovah" are repeated over and over again throughout the entire book.

He portrays the renegade apostate condition of Judah before the Captivity, and warns against the guilt of the people and the coming of the destruction of Jerusalem. But he also holds out special promises concerning the means by which the glory of the Nation is to be restored, namely, repentance and the renunciation of False Shepherds, and the acceptance of the *Good Shepherd;* who will feed the flock (Chap. 34, 11-31). Cf. Ps. 77, 20; Isa. 40,11.

His chapter number thirty-four (34) might well be called the Christ Chapter!

Ezekiel continues with his prophetic announcements of a national revival by their returning of the Glory of the Lord and the ministering of the loyal priesthood.

Again I say: If you have not yet found Christ in the Old Testament, please read again the entire Chapter 34!

Twice Ezekiel calls Christ "Son of David"—also "The Son of Man."

The Book of Daniel

The Book of Daniel is sometimes called the Book of the Apocalypse of the Old Testament, or, should we say, History in Advance; a companion to the Book of Revelation.

Daniel's career resembles that of Joseph—promoted to the highest office in the realm (2,48), upholding his spiritual life in the midst of a heathen court (6, 1). Here we find pagan idolatry against Loyalty to God; an ungoldly king's pride arrayed against Divine Sovereignty; impious sacrilege pitted against Reverence for Sacred Objects.

But Godly Wisdom wins, and the king is turned out to eat grass (4, 4-37).

We find herein also "The Handwriting on the Wall." Belshazzar dethroned (5,1-30); the contest between plotting and the Providence of God; the mouth of the lion stopped (6, 1-28).

Much of the Book of Daniel is imagery and mysterious, and any attempt to try to fit the prophecies of Daniel and Revelation into the facts of history only produces an endless conflict of opinions among Bible scholars.

One thing though is sure, and that is that Daniel's prophecies do represent a partly veiled revelation of the events to come, in secular as well as in sacred history.

The visions point to the ultimate and absolute victory and triumph of the *Bride* (Christ's Church) over all powers on earth and hell, and the final vision has to do specially with the Coming of Christ, the Messiah.

Daniel calls Christ: "The Most Holy" (9,24), and "The Ancient of Days" (7,22), see "God Eternal" (Deut.32,40). Cf. "Most High" (7,22; 9,24).

The Book of Hosea

Hosea's account of an apparent unchaste and unfaithful wife, *if* true, enables him to portray God's attitude to Israel (Neh. 1, 2-3; 2, 1-5). God, the husband (Neh. 2, 20; Isa, 54,5) and Israel, representing the indecent and unworthy wife (2, 2).

Israel's apostasy is symbolized by the experience of the prophet in his marriage (1,3); her national identity is lost, and the kingdom becomes a marred and useless vessel unto the Lord (8,8).

However, as our Lord so often said: "There are blessings and joy in repentance" (Chap. 14). Cf. Matt 9,13; Luk. 17,3. All of which leads us right back to Christ, ". . . joy shall be in heaven over one sinner that repenteth" (Luk. 15,7).

Hosea calls Christ *"Versatile"*; meaning completeness and competence in everything.

The Book of Joel

This name means "Jehovah is God." The book is fanciful, elegant and full of mercy and grace.

Joel wants national repentance in return for which he holds out joy and eternal blessings, and speaks of God's outpouring of the Holy Spirit and the ushering in of a great revival (Joel 2, 28-32). Cf. Pentecost. Acts 2,1-47; 1 Cor. 16,8.

The Book of Amos

Amos, the working man—herdsman and tree surgeon (7,14).

This book abounds in striking metaphors, for instance: The straining of God's mercy by sinners compared to the overloading of a wagon (2,13); or the pressure of duty upon the Prophet compared with the roaring of a lion in his den (3,8) or, the lack of the use of God's Word to a famine and hunger in the world (8,11,12).

Amos' method of leading his people was by *example* and instructions. His claim of being Divinely Inspired is made manifest by these words: "Thus saith the Lord"; this statement occurs forty times throughout his prophecy.

He repeatedly calls Israel to repentance; in turn promises them forgiveness, mercy and happiness.

Amos, as a prophet, was in many respects like Christ Himself: a) by *his occupation;* always working (7,14); b) *in his humility;* acknowledged his lowly origin (7,15); c) in *his method of teaching;* by illustration; d) by *his claim of divine inspiration;* "Thus saith the Lord;" e) in *being charged with treason* (7,10 and John 19, 12; f) by the *pressure of duty* (3,8 and John 9,4); g) *denouncing the selfishness of the rich* (6,4-5 and Luk. 9,4).

The Book of Obadiah

Obadiah refers us to the time when the Edomites refused Israel passage through their country (Num. 20, 14-21), and how they rejoiced over the capture of Jerusalem (1, 21). Cf. Ps. 137, 7-9.

A very short book indeed, but nevertheless relates God's special providential care over the Jews, God's Chosen race (Gen 3, 15), through whom Christ was to come; he even calls attention to the certainty of punishment upon those who would persecute them.

Too bad many of them eventually turned against Christ, only to blaspheme and renounce Him, and finally nail Him to the Cross. Cf. Mark 15,13; Luk. 23,31.

The Book of Jonah

The Book of Jonah tells us about Jonah being called by God to go and preach the gospel of Sin and Grace to the people of Nineveh; that Jonah *did* go; and what happened on his journey (1,3). Cf. 2 Kings 14, 25.

It tells how Jonah was overtaken (1,47); how he met God face-to-face even while inside the great fish (2, 1-10). Cf. Ps. 13-9,10. How he was disappointed over God's willingness to forgive (3,5,10).

The book teaches most emphatically the danger of running away from duty once God has issued the call to *go*. It shows us also how God can and will employ us as channels of *trust* even when as a matter of fact in ourselves we are of no use to either God or man in the first place.

Finally the Book of Jonah (compare Christ's, Luk.23,34) shows us the extreme all-inclusiveness and wideness of God's mercy and love.

The story about the large fish that provided board and room for a fugitive bigot for three days, has been (and still is) ridiculed and mocked, especially by such as believe only what they see with their closed eyes and hold in their soiled hands!

Really, though, what difference does it make whether the fish swallowed Jonah, or Jonah swallowed the fish? *If* the Bible said that Jonah swallowed the fish, *then I would believe that;* though I would not understand. When God could make heaven and earth and all things in a short time, He could also make a fish (any size needed) in order to carry out His eternal plan for Jonah.

Remember this too: The Jews, God's chosen people, from whom and through whom Christ was to come—*they;* to whom God had given the responsibility to *keep God's records straight for all time; they* believed in the story of Jonah, otherwise it would *never* have been entered in the Scriptures!!! And, Jesus Christ *himself* believed *all* of the Scriptures, including the Book of Jonah and *did quote* from that book (Matt. 12, 39-41; Luk. 11, 29-30. Read specially Matthew 12, 39-41!).

"How can these things be?" That's the question Nicedemus put to Jesus (John 3,9).

That same question the devil uses continually in his attempt to make us mistrust The Scriptures, and set aside God's eternal plan of our salvation.

Take the case of Jonah and the great fish; that's an easy one because it's so reasonable to deny it as a miraculous fact. The unbeliever would have us believe that this occurrence is a good novel and an imaginary event, but that it actually never did happen.

They say it's good if you are interested in mission work, because it has the tendency to hold out the idea that God does forgive sin. Cf. Jonah 3, 4-10; Matt. 12, 41. A real good "story" they say.

To throw this right back into their face—Does it really make any difference who swallowed who? If God had said that Jonah swallowed the fish then of course genuine faith would accept that (Gen. 17, 1; Ex. 6, 3; 2 Cor. 6, 18). For HE who suffered, died and rose again holds the key to both heaven and hell (Rev. 1, 18, 20, 1, Cf. Deut. 32, 29; Ps. 68, 20).

Did it ever occur to you doubters that God wants us to accept the Jonah-Fish incident as an eventful and adventurous happening, standing by itself as a historical fact, yet leading us onward into a series of tragic events that terminates episodically with the rising of our Lord and Savior from His tomb? If not then why did Christ Himself repeatedly refer to the event and thus tie it into His resurrection from the dead? The fish and the tomb, the empty fish and the empty grave go hand in hand just as do the law and the gospel. They can never be separated, in this world or the next.

All this of course the Scribes and Pharisees rejected most vehemently, always plotting to kill our Lord and Savior. (Matt. 12,14,25). Cf. Matt. 27, 1; Mark 3,6; Luk. 6,11; John 5, 18.

But before we proceed let us first determine who the Pharisees were, and why our Lord repeatedly called them a "generation of vipers," and an "evil and adulterous generation"?

The name "Pharisee" means to be separated from all mankind by special works, especially such as refused to have anything to do with the Levitical system (anti Christ, for short).

Their influence was very great, and they ruled beyond any question the entire Sanhedrin (the court of final appeal and last resort) as well as all Jewish society.

And why did they call Jesus "MASTER?" Because they no doubt used the title as a most derogatory and degrading manner, judging and condemning Him in hate and anger supreme. Math. 9, 11.

And who were the Sadducees? They were a small, but wealthy and influencial Jewish sect, and a very determined adversary of our Lord and Savior. They absolutely denied the divinity of the oral Law, and they did not believe at all in the resurrection of the dead (nor Christ's) nor in angels (Matt. 22,23). Cf. Matt. 16,12. In this respect they were much like some of the many who today call themselves "pastors" and "professors of excellence."

Supposing now that we call in our main witness in the case and see what HE has to say?

When the Pharisees and scribes demanded a sign (miracle) from Jesus He told them frankly that the only miracle for them would be the "THREE DAYS IN THE BELLY, AND THE THREE DAYS IN THE GRAVE" miracle—"for as Jonah was three days and three nights in the whale's belly; SO shall the Son of man be three days and three nights in the heart of the earth." (Matt. 12,40) Cf. Matt. 16,21.

Now tell me this: If Christ Himself did not want to tie the Jonah-Fish episode into His own rising from the dead, then WHY did He so OFTEN keep on referring to it, time and time again? From the very first: "From that time forth Began Jesus to shew unto his disciples, how that He must go unto Jerusalem, and suffer many things of the elders and chief priests and scribes, and be killed, AND BE RAISED AGAIN THE THIRD DAY" (Matt. 16, 21).

After telling his disciples about His own passion to come, He concluded: "Tell the vision to no man (the transfiguration), until the Son of man be risen from the dead" (Matt. 17, 9).

"And while they abode in Galilee, Jesus said unto them, the Son of man shall be betrayed unto the hands of men; and they shall kill Him, and the third day he shall be raised again" (Matt. 17,23).

Subsequent to telling His disciples about the parable of the labourers Christ also told them how He would be mocked, scourged and crucified, and "THE THIRD DAY HE SHALL RISE AGAIN." (Matt. 20,19).

Our Lord and Savior even went so far as to tell them about this in the most emphatic words: "BUT AFTER I am risen, I will go before you into Galilee (Matt. 26, 32). Cf. 28, 7, 16.

Even the false witnesses (during the trial) said: "This fellow said, I am able to destroy the temple of God, and to build it in three days" (Matt. 26, 61) Cf. Matt. 27, 40; John 2, 19.

Even while Christ was hanging on the cross people could not leave Him in peace, but walked by, reviling Him, wagging their heads, and saying: "Thou that destroyest the temple and buildest it in three days, save thyself" (Matt. 27, 39, 40).

And now comes the great climax of the Jonah-Fish miracle, when Joseph took the rejected body of our Lord and Savior and laid it in his own new tomb, which had been hewn out of solid rock (THE ROCK BURIED IN A ROCK), while very special Mary Magdaline was sitting by.

But not even now, after Christ did rise from the grave, would they leave Him alone, but had to come to Pilate and remind him too that: "THIS DECEIVER said, (while He was still alive) AFTER THREE DAYS I WILL RISE AGAIN." Matt. 27, 63). Cf. Matt. 16, 21.

So then, after all, Christ WAS RISEN, and when an angel from heaven rolled back the stone, Pilate's guards became as dead men. (Matt. 28, 4). To Mary, the angel said: "hurry, go and tell his disciples that he is risen from the dead." (Matt. 28, 7).

Three times after His rising from the grave did Jesus appear before the eleven disciples (Judas having gone to his place), and now, even Thomas believed. DO YOU?

Then (now) a word about miracles in general, to wit:

A miracle is an act or happening in the material or physical sphere that departs from the laws of nature and goes far beyond what is known concerning these laws; occuring in such a way as to call attention to the nearness, the controlling power and eternal will of the Living God.

Miracles are not opposed to nature, though they *are* opposed to what we know about nature.

The appearance of angels, so often mentioned in the Bible,

strictly speaking, are not the same as the miracles of which my notations subsequently herein speak; nor is the miracle of our conversion the same.

For instance: The miracle that elevates our sinful soul from damnation to salvation, while it is caused by a supernatural effect in the unseen world, it does have a visible result in the world of nature (a complete change in our heart), and, consequently is a much greater miracle than any physical miracle performed by Christ our Lord during His mission on earth, nevertheless, it is not a miracle in the sense heretofore mentioned.

I know, you know, that miracles happen right before our eyes every day, as for instance people rescued from death and danger; miracles of healing (not by quacks); miracles of fortitude; miracles of example, and other remarkable events.

But in this article let us confine ourselves to the miracles of the Bible, referred to in Holy Writ as "Signs," "wonders," "Power," and or "Mighty Works" of God.

There are many miracles (performed) accounted for in God's Word; some forty-four in the Old Testament, happening in Egypt, in the wilderness, in Canaan, under various kings, by Elijah, by Elisha, by (recorded by) Isaiah, during the captivity, etc., etc.; but mostly by Moses and Aaron.

In the New Testament we find the record of some thirty-six miracles performed by our Lord, twenty of which are recorded by St. Matthew, eighteen by St. Mark, 21 by St. Luke, and eight by St. John.

St. John records six miracles witnessed by *none* of the other three evangelists; whereas the feeding of the five thousand is recorded by all four evangelists (the only miracle being thus "honored").

The Old Testament miracles were performed by Moses and Aaron; by Joshua; by Samson; by a certain prophet of Judah; by Elijah; by Elisha; and (recorded) by Isaiah.

In the New Testament miracles were performed by our Lord Himself (for the most part); but also by Peter, by Paul; and by the Disciples (and apostles); by Stephen; by Philip; and, by the Seventy (disciples).

Both Peter and Paul also raised people from death to life.

All the Bible miracles are listed, either by alphabetical order or by chronological arrangement in mostly all Bible concordances; and should we not take time to review them all and really study them in detail? I think this would not only strengthen our intellect and our powers of learning, but it would fortify and support our Christian Faith to the extent and degree that we will more and more come to realize the full meaning of *why* all the Bible miracles were performed.

It is true, and *you know it;* that every Bible miracle is directly or indirectly associated with and refers to the promise of a Savior to come, that He Did come; that He came only for ONE purpose and that was to fulfill the Law and the Gospel (He *is* the Gospel); that He did suffer and die in our stead; that He did rise from the grave; that He ascended to heaven; and that he *will come again!*

The Book of Micah

Micah, like so many of the other Prophets, bitterly condemns the sins of Israel as a whole, specially the greedy princes and priests who lived on captured prey.

Then too there was idolatry (1,7; 5,13); covetousness (2,2); witchcraft (5,12); treachery (7,5,6); and universal corruption (7,2-4).

"Therefore shall Zion for your sake be plowed under like a field, and Jerusalem shall become heaps" (Mic. 3,12).

But Micah also holds out real hope for his people who repent of their evil ways, and refers them to God who "pardeneth iniquity, and passeth by transgression of the remnant of his heritage. He retaineth not His anger forever, because He delighteth in mercy" (Mic. 7,18).

In Chapter Five, Micah prophesies the birthplace of Christ (5,2). Cf. also Old Testament prophecies regarding the coming of

Christ (Ps. 89,20; Deut. 18,15; Gen. 49,10; Dan. 2,44; Mal. 4,2; Num. 24,17).

Micah calls Christ, "The Judge of Israel" (5,1) and "The Ruler of Israel" (5,20).

The Book of Nahum

The Book of Nahum is said to be sort of a sequel to the Book of Jonah, its main theme being the destruction of Nineveh.

It appears that the Assyrians (Ninevites), after the Jonah episode, soon relapsed again into gross idolatry. They plundered other nations, and their own capital became like a lion's den full of prey (2, 11, 12). So Nahum pronounces Divine Vengeance upon the bloody city, yet holds out hope for their future (2,1; 1, 13-15) and refers them to Christ in these words: "Behold upon the mountains the feet of Him who bringeth forth good tidings" (Nah. 1,15).

The Book of Habakkuk

The first two chapters of this book are mainly composed of a dialogue between Habakkuk and Jehovah.

The Prophet complains to God that he sees sinful violence on every hand, yet, as is usually the procedure of all the Prophets, seeks no punishment, but trembles at God's majestic greatness and willingness to pardon. Then receives a reply revealing a Divine plan of using the Chaldeans as a swift and terrible instrument of judgment upon the wicked (1, 5-11).

But sin and shame continue. Habakkuk is not satisfied, but God encourages him to wait and see.

Then follows the sentence that has been a perpetual watchword for the Christian Church: "The just shall live by faith"—the Morning Star of the Reformation (2,4). Cf. John 3,36; Rom. 1,17.

Finally the Prophet declares his unwaivering trust in God's divine plan (2, 1-19), and great triumph for our missions (2,14); the all-conquering faith (3, 17-18).

Examples of faith: Caleb, Num. 13,30; Shadrack, Meshach and Abednego, Dan,3,17; Daniel, Dan. 6, 10; Ninevites, Jon. 3,5; etc.

The Book of Zephaniah

Here we find a Prophet that is said to have been associated in his work with Hulda, the Prophetess (2 Kings 22, 14; 2 Chron. 34, 22).

The book is exceedingly somber in its tone, and is filled with threatenings and denunciations; but the sun breaks through in the last chapter, and the Prophet foretells the Coming of a Glad Day, when Israel shall become famous throughout all the earth (Chap. 3,14-20).

Here we have a repetition of what takes place throughout all the Old Testament—first sin and shame condemned to the bottom of hell followed by pardon and forgiveness for those who repent and accept God's eternal goodness and mercy—"*Law and Gospel*" over and over again!

The Prophet Haggai

Haggai, the Prophet of the Temple. He rebukes the people for neglecting to rebuild the Temple (1,4), coupled with cheering promises to those who would undertake the work (3,11; 12,15).

Haggai tells his people of the "Appearing of the Messiah" when the glory of the Lord would fill the House of God (2,7-9). Cf. Mal. 2,7; 3,1; Luk. 2, 12.

Haggai calls Christ: "The Desire of All Nations" (2,7).

The Book of Zechariah

The Prophet of Long Vision. He wrote several of the Psalms. His prophecies concern eight visions. There are *vast* Messianic elements in his prophecies, and he tells of Christ's appearance (14, 4), how He will be manifested in lowliness (9,9); calls Him The Prince of Peace (0,20); tells of Him being crucified (12,10); Cf. Ps. 62,11; John 19,34; how the shepherd is being foresaken by his sheep (13,7). Cf. John 10,30; 14, 10, 11. He calls Christ "My Fellow" (13,7); "the Builder of the Temple" (6,13); "The Branch" (3, 8;6,12); "Shepherd of the Lord" (11,16;13,7); "My Shepherd" (13,7); "King of Zion" (9,9); "Lord." (14,3); "King over The Earth" (14,9).

The Book of Malachi

The first five chapters of Malachi deal with a dialogue between Jehovah and his people.

He paints a graphic picture of the closing period of the Old Testament history, showing that great reforms are needed in order to prepare the way for the Coming Messiah.

He reveals the sins of the ungrateful people and the priesthood; and how they fail to respond to Divine Love (1,2); how they dishonor God's name (1, 6) by presenting blemished offerings and how the priest, by their example are becoming stumbling blocks instead of spiritual leaders (2,1-8).

The better side of the picture he paints is God's glorious promise of the Coming of the Messenger of the Covenant (3, 1-4) and the outpouring of a *great blessing* (3, 10-12); the Saints becoming Jehovah's peculiar Treasure (3, 6-18), and the Dawning New Day in which righteousness shall triumph (4,2,3), and the appearance of a Spiritual Reform before the Day of the Lord is ushered in (4,5,6).

Malachi calls Christ: "The Sun of Righteousness" (Mal. 4,2; Luk. 1,78; Eph. 5,14); "The Message of the Covenant" (Mal. 3,1; Isa. 63,9; Matt. 11,10; Mk. 1,2; Luk. 1,76).

There are in the Old Testament a great many prophecies concerning the Coming and work of Christ (besides seven in the Psalms and sixteen in Isaiah). See also Gen. 3,15; 12,3; 49,10; Deut. 18,15; Jer. 23,5; Ezek. 17,22; Dan. 2, 34,44; 7,13; Mi. 5,2; Hag. 2,7; Zech. 3,8; 6,12; 9,9; 11,12; 12;10; 13,7; Mal. 3,1.

Summing up the whole matter in a few words, it's always the same, always was and always will be, sin and grace, wickedness and pardon, Law and Gospel—**that's the Bible in a nutshell.**

This manifests itself throughout all of the Old Testament. The people were bad, very bad. Individuals, groups of people, cities, entire nations were utterly destroyed because of their sinful life and because they refused to walk in the ways of the Lord. On the other hand God never lacked in love and pardon for all who came to Him (if they did); and at the end of every day of condemnation there we always find that God held the door open *if* they wanted to come in.

Might we now not divide the issue in three short parts, to wit: *First;* the *Law* is simply a Scriptural doctrine wherein God's justice is exposed to us in all its fierceness and fury. In this *Law* God is fully revealed to us; and *because* of our evil thoughts, words and deeds (including lack of faith) and our secret sins thrown in for good measure, the *Law* becomes for us an expression of imminent danger and potential penalty for violations of God's rules and conduct.

Second; the GOSPEL on the other hand, shows us the antithetical side of the Law. It makes evident by Holy Writ and Scriptural procedure that regardless of our sins, great or small, there *is* hope and forgiveness for all who confess their sins and accept, that is, receive without doubt, the Son of God as their Lord and Savior, a most singular gift, without any merit or excellence on our part whatsoever.

Most of us have received a pat on the back or some sort of an "Award of Merit" during out span of life. But redemption, that is the Gospel, knows of no rewards for conduct; here no competitive examinations are permitted. The Gospel, eternal life, is *free*.

Third; And herewith comes the difficult part, should I say, the hard to understand part. It is here that we learn that the Law and the Gospel go hand in hand. We cannot have one without the other. It is true that love and mercy were Christ's great purpose, and that healing and forgiveness were marked by every step that He took. There was indeed concentration and fragrance in every word that He spoke, blessings and pleasure in all the deeds he performed.

Nevertheless, Christ was as consistent as He was kind and generous, and *repeatedly* He said: "Repent, Repent!" He even *cursed* such as lack charity with everlasting fire in company with the devil and his angels. (Matt. 25,41. See also—Mark 9, 41-48.

So, the difference between the Law and the Gospel then consists only in a limited sense. They are much alike in this that they are both to be found in the New Testament as well as in the Old Testament. And in no way are they contentious; that is, the one does not contradict the other; they never argue!

That is exactly what I have attempted to show in the foregoing brief elucidations herewith submitted to you for your most worthy consideration.

No matter how we try to explain the various doctrines in the Old Testament we can come up with just *one* solution, and that is that God continually manifested His most violent anger and extreme indignation over the sins of the people; but, in practically every book of the Old Testament (before the day is over) God's Prophets always held out hope of forgiveness and mercy if the people will only confess their sins, mend their evil ways, and accept the *promise* that the Messiah *will come*.

With this in mind then we must proclaim that there *does exist* between Law and Gospel a unity and *oneness;* an absolute fellowship and companionship which is complete and inclusive in the fullest possible sense of the word.

Nothing can be accomplished, however, by turning to God for help until we first come to know ourselves as sinners, without hope. The thought of forgiveness finds no comfort in a heart filled with iniquities and injustice.

So we turn to the Gospel (whether it be the Old or New Testament (Cf. Gen. 3, 15; 12,3; 49,10; Deut. 18,15; Jer. 23,5; Ezek. 17, 22; Dan. 2,34, 44; 7,13; Mic. 5,2; Hag. 2,7; Zech. 3,8; 6, 12; 9,9; 11, 12; 12, 10;13, 7; Mal. 3, 1) wherein God actually proclaims to a sin-cursed world His eternal Love, Mercy and Grace, a proclamation that not only offers but actually *brings* forgiveness and pardon and forever takes away all desires and justifiable intentions on the part of God to turn His back on us.

Immortality

In the Old Testament immortality was (is) taken for granted, bestowed and conferred by sanction and obedience to the Holy Writings.

David speaks at length of immortality when he says: "your length of days are forever" (Ps. 21, 4); "your heart shall live forever" (22, 26); and, "I will dwell in the house of the Lord forever" (23, 6); and, "God will redeem my soul from the power of the grave" (49, 15); and, "Thou hast delivered my soul from death... that I may walk before God in the light of the living" (56, 13); and, "The children of Thy servants shall continue, and their seed shall be established before Thee" (102, 28).

Moses says (may have been Agur or Lemuel): "The wicked is driven away in his wickedness; but the righteous hath hope in his death" (Prov. 14, 32).

"Thy dead men shall live; together with my dead body shall they arise. Awake and sing, ye that dwell in dust, for thy dew is as the dew of herbs, and the earth shall cast out the head" (Isa. 26,29).

"And many of them that sleep in the dust of the earth shall awake, some to everlasting life, and some to everlasting shame and everlasting contempt. And they that be wise shall shine as the brightness of the firmanent; and they that turn many to righteousness as the stars for ever and ever" (Dan. 12, 2, 3). See also Prov. 4, 18; Matt. 25,46; John 5,28; Acts 24,15; James 5,20; etc. etc.

I sometime wonder what the Lord will say when on the *last day* He takes a final look at the smart alecky, offensively conceited "leaders" in our church who have knowingly and willingly turned our people AWAY from righteousness into the paths of their impenetrable wicked teaching!!

Will they then "shine as stars in the brightness of truth"? I wonder!

WHY are they so utterly cocky and jauntily conceited? Is it because of their super intelligence that they misunderstand the mysteries of God? Why do they not believe THOUGH THEY DO NOT UNDERSTAND? Cf. John 20, 29; 2 Cor. 5, 7; 1 Pet. 1, 8.

"Fructu non arborem estima" (Judge a tree by its fruit, not by its leaves).

So, we continue with the New Testament, and see what we can learn there about immortality.

Paul says: "To them who by patient continuance in well doing seek for glory and honor and immortality, eternal life" etc. (Rom. 2,7). (Will you now also please read all of 1 Cor. 15, 43-48).

Together with God we too are immortal as God Himself is *immortal* (1 Tim. 1, 16, 17; 6, 16; Acts 22,18).

In his letter to Timothy Paul says: "But is now made manifest by the appearing of our Lord Jesus Christ, who hath abolished death, and hath brought life and immortality to light through the Gospel (2 Tim. 1, 10). Cf. 1 Cor. 15, 54.

Christ Himself (lest we believe not Paul) says: "And fear not them which kill the body, but are not able to kill the soul; but rather fear him which is able to destroy both soul and body in hell" (Matt. 10, 28). Cf. Isa. 8, 12, 13; Luk. 12,4.

Elsewhere Christ continues: "And everyone that hath forsaken houses, and brethern, and sisters, or fathers, or mothers, or wife and children, or lands, for my sake, shall receive an hundredfold; and shall inherit everlasting life" (Matt. 19, 29). Cf. Mark 10,29,30; Luk. 18,29,30.

In speaking of the unkind and selfish person Christ says: "They shall go away into everlasting punishment; but the righteous (those who manifest their faith by good will and mercy) shall have life eternal" (Matt. 25,46). Cf. Dan. 12,2; John 5,29; Rom. 2,7. etc. etc.

Paul declares most emphatically that "it is manifest by the appearance of our Lord Jesus Christ, who abolished death, and has brought life and immortality to light THROUGH THE GOSPEL" (2 Tim. 1,10). that, "this corruptible must put on incorruption," and, that "this mortal must put on *immortality* (1 Cor. 15,53). Cf. 2 Cor. 5,4.

Our body (originally created in the image of God) is indeed most wonderful and complete in every detail.

But we also have a soul, an *immortal* soul, the essence of which is spiritual. Its element or composition no man can understand. It abides in the body, though it takes up neither room nor space. Not only the soul itself is a mystery, but *immortality too* and (though this should not excite our curiosity in the least) is a Scriptural *fact* that must be accepted in faith and faith alone.

Whatever we understand (or do not understand) about the life immortal one thing we may be sure of (Scripture gives us that promise) and that is that for the soul there is no death, because it is divinely imperishable and sacrosanctly inviolable. This I *believe;* "Because the Bible tells me so"!

Though our body *must die* decay and return to dust (Gen. 3, 19; Eccl. 3, 20); the illustrous individuality and personality of the soul can *never* change, but will continue to exist as a distinct and singular reality *forever;* either together with God in heavenly glory; or, in hell together with the devil.

Parables

There are also eleven Parables in the Old Testament, and I list them as follows:

1) The trees that went forth one at a time (Judg. 9,7-15); 2) Nathan's effect on David (2 Sam. 12,1-5); 3) One of Tekoah's sons killed the other son (2 Sam. 14,4-6); 4) Ahab's life pays for another life (1 Kings 20,39-42); 5) The thisstle and the cedar (2 Kings 14, 9); 6) Two kings see each other face to face (2 Chron. 25, 27, 18); 7) The vineyard with wild grapes (Isa. 5, 1-8); 8) The marred girdle (Jer. 13, 1-11); 9) Two eagles and the vine (Ezek. 17, 1-10); 10) Israel—The Captured Lion (Ezek. 19, 2-9); 11) The boiling pot (Ezek. 24, 1-5).

As before stated, our Lord and Savior often spoke by parables, and, if you do not mind I beg you to permit me to bother you with just one of my own parables, hoping that you will continue to *find Christ in the Old Testament* as well as in the New Testament. The parable follows herewith: *The Girl That Knew It All.*

Sixty years ago, in Texas, a little girl, Salonica Rosario, age nine, came to me one day and said: "Mr. Holt, my teacher is pregnant; but our principal says she can teach until the seventh month of her pregnancy."

Said I to her: "How come you know so much about things like this at your age?" To this she replied: "I can see, can't I. "And besides," she said, "according to what my two teenage sisters tell me, in about three years, I, personally, will have a great surprise coming up."

Then I said to her: "Since you are so extraordinarily smart, let me now ask you a few questions to give you a chance to prove your intellect also along other lines"; to which she replied: "Shoot away, old boy."

My first question was: "How long can a dumb duck stand on one foot?" "Try it and see for yourself,'" she said. Then I said: "Tell me two ways to use the word 'sow' "; her sarcastic reply was: "Feed your female pigs well; but first 'sow' your oats (feed)."

BY THIS TIME SALONICA IS 15 YEARS OLD

And I continue to ask her questions. Said I to her: "When we speak of timbre, to what do we refer?" "To music, of course," was her reply.

While on that subject I asked her to name me four reed instruments used in her school band; and these are the ones she named: "clarinet, saxophone, bassoon, and sax-tuba."

"How about the strings," I said, "can you name me four such instruments?" to which she replied: "Violin, banjo, guitar, and ukelele." Then I thought I would give her a real tough one, and I asked her to name me at least four percussion instruments; and her quick-as-a-wink reply was: "The cymbals, drums, xylophone, and the tambourine."

BY THIS TIME SALONICA IS 24

She is half way into college life, and her intellectuality continues to expand and multiply by leaps and bounds. She carries 23 credits, such as biology, cosmography, conchology, radiobiology, geophysics, etc., and she knows all about snails, oysters, cattlefish and their shells; and she knows all about gelsemium and the entire group of twining shrubs.

She knows all about weather, winds, and tides, and their effect on the earth; she knows all about optical activity and the ability of certain substances to rotate the plane of polarization when transmitting polarized light; she knows everything there is to know about the opsonic index, that is, the ratio of the number of bacteria destroyed by phagocytes in the individual's blood serum to the number destroyed in a normal blood serum.

College life is *great;* for Salonica, and her wisdom will soon go beyond that of King Solomon! Oh yes, already she knows all about the intensity and actinic power of solar radiation; she knows all there is to know about scapalamine, a vegetable alkaloid used to produce dilation of the pupil of the eye; and don't you know, too, she knows all about the actinonzoa, a class of the Poelenterata, a sea animal whose body consists essentially of a stomach divided into chambers.

AN HONORARY UNIVERSITY GRADUATE, AGE 34

Care, prudence, circumspection, caution, forethought, frugality and providence (based on self-will); that's what Salonica, all these years has striven for, and *received*.

Her vast earthly knowledge continues; "round and round she goes, and where she stops, nobody knows."

She knows all about Achitophel, a character in Dryden's poetic satire, a caricature in (Drama) "Lord Shaflesbury." She also knows all about the large, northern constellation, its three brightest stars forming, together with one star from the constellation Andromeda, the square of Pegasus, known as the "winged horse"; and all about Antares, a red star of the first magnitude, the brightest star in the Scorpio constellation.

NOW COMES THE DARK CLOUDS IN THE HORIZON

No matter *how much* Salonica knows about God's most wonderful creation she seems to have forgotten all about Him who made it all (Eccl. 12, 1; Isa. 40, 28; Rom. 1, 25; I Pet. 4, 10), even the stars, including the "Morning Star" (Christ Jesus) who brought us *the Light of the Gospel* (Rev. 22, 16). Cf. Num. 24,17; Matt. 2, 2.

She does not even mention the *star* that guided and guarded the Magi on their way to Bethlehem, that most *gracious of all nights* when Jesus of Nazareth was born (Matt. 2, 9); *"His star"*; in the East (Matt. 2, 2)!

Salonica knows all about Oriental agallochum (aloes), but did it ever occur to her that when David describes for us the majesties of heaven, the "oil of gladness," and the "smell of aloes" will make us happy? (Ps. 45, 7, 8). Cf. S.S. 1, 3.

Strange—Salonica, even at the age of 9, knew the names of the *four* string instruments, the *four* reed instruments, and the *four* percussions used in her high school band. But now, white haired and wrinkled faced, even now, she does not know the names of the *four* evangelists who wrote the *four Gospels;* nor has she said one word as to what these gospels contain.

She knew all about radium A, a substance formed from radon (step by step) by atomic disintegration, which by further (step by step) disintegration gives rise to radium B, which in turn (step by step) gives rise to radium C; etc., etc. But in all her wisdom we find *no trace* of (step by step) sin and grace; (step by step) confession and forgiveness; and no (step by step) *Law and Gospel.*

AND NOW OUR ERUDITE SALONICA IS 84

My poor old lady. She knew *so much* that it would take a freight train with 110 box cars and a bright red caboose to carry all her knowledge and wisdom; and *yet* she knew so *very little!*

My poor Salonica; *My Poor Salonica.*

"Magna est veritas et praevalebit"—Great is truth and it will prevail.

Life Hereafter

The Old Testament continually emphasizes the *eternal destiny* of God's chosen people. Where can we ever find anything more beautiful than what God says in Isaiah 43, 8-13? If this is not *Gospel;* Old Testament Gospel in all its fullness and glory. "I, am the Lord; and beside me there is no Savior."

"The people that walked in darkness have seen a great light; they that dwell in the land of the shadow of death, upon them hath the light shined. . . For unto us a child is born, unto us a son is given; and the government shall be upon his shoulder; and his name shall be called Wonderful, Counsellor, The Mighty God, The Everlasting Father, The Prince of Peace" (Isa. 9, 2, 6).

"Therefore the Lord Himself shall give you a sign; Behold, a virgin shall conceive, and bear a son, and shall call his name Immanuel" (Isa. 7, 14).

And then comes the *Law: the Day of Jehovah;* when all the world will be judged in righteousness: "Howl, ye; for the day of the Lord at at hand; it shall come as a destruction from the Almighty" (Isa. 13, 6); "Behold, the day of the Lord cometh cruel both with wrath and fierce anger, to lay the land desolate; and he shall destroy the sinner thereof out of it" (Isa. 13, 9).

"Put ye in the sickle, for the harvest is ripe; come, get you down, for the press is full, the fats overflow; for their wickedness is great" (Joel, 3, 13). "The day of God's wrath is near" (Zeph. Chapter 1.)!

And as I have repeated so often in the past; we can not have the Gospel without also having the Law (nor the Law without the Gospel). The two go hand in hand, always. They come in pairs!

And we do not have to go to the New Testament to find out that our body eventually *must die;* decay, and return to dust (Gen. 3, 19; Eccl. 3, 20); the illustrious individuality and personality of the soul can *never* change, but will continue to exist as a distinct and singular reality *forever;* either together with God in heavenly glory; or, in hell together with the devil and his angels.

"Veni, vidi, vici" (I came, I saw, I conquered).

In the name of my Lord and Savior, Jesus Christ, Amen, Amen.

Addenda

Christ in the **Old Testament,** all the way!

Whatever happened in the life or development of the **Old Testament** people would not have happened had it not been for Christ.

All the narrations, stories, and history in the **Old Testament** would never had been recorded were it not for Christ.

All the **Old Testament** confusion and strife, all the conflicts and hostilities between people, tribes and nations would be unheard of were it not for Christ.

All the **Old Testament** military operations as a science or a profession (or should we say just plain slaughter of women and children by the millions) would never have happened were it not for Christ.

In fact all **Old Testament** false doctrine, idolatry and the killing of God's prophets would never have taken place were it not for Christ.

Briefly stated Christ had to take the blame for it all. He was right in the middle all the way from: "In the beginning God" (Gen. 1,1), to: "See, I will send you [John] another, a prophet like Elijah before the coming of the great and dreadful *Judgment Day of God*. His preaching will bring fathers and children together again, to be of one mind and heart, for they will know that if they do not repent, I will come and utterly destroy their land" (Mal. 4, 5-6). Cf. Matt. 17, 10-12; Luk. 1, 17.

And for all the humiliation, suffering, and death brought to Christ (The Son of God), all He got out of it was to be nailed to the criminal's cross, hated by all men, and rejected by his own *Father* (Matt. 27, 46). All this was foretold by God's prophets in the OLD TESTAMENT!

Time for Prayer

Merciful and gracious Father in heaven, hear my humble cry! Have pity on me, and take away all my transgressions. Wash away my sin and make me clean again.

I confess that I daily sin against Thee, and this bothers me every day of my life. Every night before bedtime I crawl on my elbows and knees across the floor in my bedroom in penitence and sorrow, not only because I *HAVE* seriously offended Thee, but because I actually *WANTED* to commit sin against You.

I admit that I was conceived and born in sin; but I also know that in the cleansing power of the blood of your Son, my Savior and Lord, there is *cleansing power supreme* for all who believe that we can and *will* be forgiven, and that our wicked past will be forgotten forever.

Merciful and gracious Father in heaven, please create in me a new and clean heart, and fill it with noble thoughts and righteous desires.

Restore unto me again true joy and the actual feeling of your salvation; *then;* and only then, will I be able to guide others unto the highways of life that lead to everlasting happiness and peace.

Amen, Amen. Cf. Psalm 51.